"As sales managers, our job is to help sales people understand their 'blindspots.' We want to help them recognize these barriers to their ability to maximize their performance. Ironically, it is often our own blindspots as managers that adversely impact what we seek to achieve with our people. In his book, Blindspots, Mark vividly illustrates this problem in our own behaviors, and clearly identifies how we can eliminate them, connecting effectively and impactfully with our people. Blindspots is an outstanding guide to help managers get out of their own way and develop their people."

— Dave Brock, Author, *Sales Manager's Survival Guide*, and President of Partners in Excellence

"The timing couldn't be better for me. With a whole new team of resellers I need to take inventory of my biases and how I'm coming across to them. I plan to practice humility intentionally and find a coach or two for 2019. While the funnel process content is valuable, the Blindspots' observations and examples were priceless. What sales leader shouldn't read this book? No one I can think of. Well done!"

— John Hoskins, Founder and Author of Level 5 Selling

"Mark has created a framework for helping others achieve what THEY desire to achieve (true coaching). Very lofty stuff. Blindspots *is really difference making work here.*"

— Mitch Little VP Global Sales and Applications, Microchip Technology

D1518295

"Mark Sellers has done it again, raising the bar in sales thinking, this time for sales management. In his new book Blindspots, Mark gives us a practical strategy for raising performance that any sales leader can grasp and put into practice. Share Blindspots with your team— then sit back and watch the results as each sales leader becomes indispensable to the growth of your company."
— Tom Heinmiller, Sales Consultant

"Just like a collision avoidance system protects your car from objects in your blind spot, Mark's book, Blindspots, will protect your sales managers from their blindspots in coaching their sales teams."
— Jim Arbuckle, President, Royal Brass and Hose

"Mark's approach to understanding our customers' buying process has given me tremendous insight to our current sales performance and his 1:1 coaching of my sales management team has meaningfully enhanced our future sales potential."
— Kenneth Escoe, Group President ITW

"I knew Mark's Funnel Principle was provocative when I discovered him speaking at a Trane conference. He turned the sales funnel upside down. Now, in Blindspots, he's done it again. He turns sales coaching inside out."
— Kris Hardin, Vice President Hunton Services, an Independent Trane Franchise

"Mark has inspired me as a leader by writing about and demonstrating the strength of vulnerability in his recent book, Blindspots. This book is a classic 'what to do and what not to do' as it demonstrates the impact that can be had when leaders focus on influencing behavior as a means of influencing results."
— Bryant Hope, Director of Sales ITW Commercial Construction North America

"This book will surprise you with many gems: its counterintuitive perspective on the challenges of data and transparency, the types of sales managers and blindspots and how to get out of your own way, the power of emotional connection to fuel relationships and coaching effectiveness, and more. Most importantly, for me, is the power of the BuyCycle Funnel™ for helping salespeople sell better by focusing on where the customer is in the decision making cycle. Frankly, Mark has been flipping the funnel for years, and it's time for the sales profession to pay closer attention. I'd recommend this book for this reason alone, but as I've mentioned, there's plenty more, weaved into a myriad of relatable stories and analogies that make it a quick and easy read, for something with so much value."

— Mike Kunkle, Vice President of Sales Enablement Services, SPASIGMA America

"Every year we layer on complexity to the role of the sales manager without taking anything off. As a sales leader myself, I can attest that the process of prioritizing our efforts to help our teams drive results is mystical at best. Rather than focus on theory, Blindspots provides practical guidance around the power of data available in all organizations, how to organize that data into meaningful patterns, and most importantly, how we can get out of our own way and create a path towards success when coaching our sellers."

— Jon Hodge, President Advantage Performance Group

"Blindspots delivers a unique perspective through the lens of a professional sales coach, Mark Sellers. His experiences with my sales leaders and their teams over several years has provided keen insight into behaviors and performance. In Blindspots we learn the journey that Mark has traveled that gives him this uniquely personal perspective that so many sales leaders can benefit from."

— Darin Lyon, President Anderson & Vreeland

"Mark's latest work, Blindspots, is a great reminder of the complex human relationships we encounter in coaching a sales team. Mark does a great job illustrating the areas where we as leaders tend to get stuck. His input and guidance into my business is very valuable and it's no surprise that his book is equal to that standard. Blindspots will be worth your time to read."
> — Andy Gillis, General Manager, Provident Inc.

"I've trusted Mark in front of my clients as a coach/trainer and am particularly impressed with his care and interest in sales leadership. He has a knack for getting sales leaders to buy into new processes. He's collaborative instead of prescriptive. In Blindspots, Mark shows where he gets this compassion from and explains how any sales leader who's determined to get better can do so."
> — Bennett Phillips, Consultant, Advantage Performance Group

"In Blindspots, Mark walks the walk about making an emotional connection with people. He's honest, transparent and vulnerable— things he encourages sales managers to be in order to create their own emotional connections with their salespeople. These emotional connections create motivated salespeople, and motivated salespeople will hit quota."
> — Gary Ross, CEO Ross Innovations, and author of The Growth Cube

"Mark brings timeless direction and a way of thinking into the present sales condition. I have long been a believer in Mark's work so much that we partner with him with our clients. Blindspots is a must read for sales leaders looking to go deeper with their teams!"
> — Steve Gran, Co-founder WorkExcellence

Blindspots

The Hidden Killer of Sales Coaching

How to Get Out of Your Own Way
And Unleash the Greatness Within

Mark Sellers

Breakthrough Sales Performance • Dublin, Ohio

MARK SELLERS

Author of the ground breaking sales book
The Funnel Principle

Sales coach to top companies
and leaders worldwide

www.breakthrough-sales.com
614.571.8267
blindspotsinsales.blog

DEDICATION

To everyone who suffered through my blindspots
for so many years, and to everyone who helped
me run my race, so far, thank you so much.

ACKNOWLEDGEMENTS

I am grateful to many people. Most of all my clients. Without your trust and faith in me with your sales managers, salespeople, VPs of Sales, GMs, directors and more, I would not have what I give — the things I have learned. You inspire me to search for the next insight.

While my beliefs and conclusions about coaching are based on observing coaching conversations between sales managers and salespeople, I have taken great care to change the names of those I've observed and coached. Any resemblance to specific companies and individuals is purely a coincidence.

Mark Sellers
August 2019

Table of Contents

Forward

After serving five years as an officer in the United States Air Force, I entered the corporate business world and worked my way up to leadership roles in manufacturing functions. I soon discovered a love for strategy, customers and deal-making and followed my instincts to the commercial side of businesses. Eventually I became a general manager.

My time running manufacturing plants and exposure to lean thinking made me see the tremendous value in process orientation. I also learned that you can't build long-term business success without sustainable sales growth. While productivity enhancements and cost savings are good things, sales growth is wonderful and desirable. I discovered that many sales professionals are not process-oriented and as a result their performance can sometimes be inconsistent. As a leader, I need steady, predictable sales performance.

It was in my first general manager assignment that I hired Mark. Since then I've retained Mark to help me raise the bar in sales performance at three assignments at Fortune 500 and private equity-owned companies where I've had global and national P&L responsibilities as the general manager. His Funnel Principle sales system has been key to me delivering on my commitments to boards, owners and other stakeholders.

Mark has also become a great friend and trusted business advisor. He's a highly ethical business man, connects well with my sales leaders, and is a great family man.

In his new book, *Blindspots: The Hidden Killer of Sales Coaching*, you'll enjoy reading Mark's time-tested and true-north principles on coaching sales people. The book has a surprise, however, as Mark gets real about truly connecting with people and looking in the mirror at yourself as a leader. Mark's riveting testimony on his self-discovery makes it hard to put this book down.

Open your mind, take some risks and apply Mark's proven approaches for real personal connections and great leadership and sales results.

Law Burks
US President Forming & Shoring
Brand Safway
January 2019

Introduction

Throughout my sales training and coaching career (23 years and counting), I have heard thousands of conversations between sales managers and their salespeople. It's a fascinating view that I am privileged to have. I thank the many clients that have hired me to listen to and then coach their managers on how to make those conversations more effective.

In these 1:1 calls, everyone dials in—the manager, the salesperson, and me. I usually say little and take lots of notes. Then the manager and I debrief after the call to reflect on one question – how effective was that conversation? After sitting in on several calls in a row by a manager I see patterns and habits emerge.

I've discovered that managers are unaware of behaviors they

consistently commit that prevent them from delivering effective coaching and developing stronger relationships with their salespeople. I call these behaviors blindspots.

Blindspots are distracting and can be demotivating for salespeople. Most of all blindspots are a problem because they can cause salespeople to underperform. It's common for the blindspots to be so bad sometimes that the salesperson leaves to go work for someone else.

Every sales manager has blindspots. If you're a sales manager, I'm going to help you become aware of them, understand them, and deal with them. You'll see your influence with your people skyrocket.

My sales training and coaching business hasn't always been this laser-focused on making sales managers better leaders. After a 12-year career selling and managing salespeople for healthcare companies, I became an independent sales consultant, selling and delivering training and consulting for a well-known global sales training company. We were good at training, but we couldn't get training to stick. We weren't any worse than any other company in that regard. The whole industry was stuck in a broken model.

After several years I left that training company and formed a new one because I was determined to fix what I saw was broken in the sales training industry. First I created a 'buying journey' sales model that helps sellers align selling to how their customers buy, called The BuyCycle Funnel™. This model has emerged as a "new standard" for selling.

Then I created a system that gets training to stick and called it Funnel Principle Selling. I implemented it with several companies, and then wrote a book about it called, *The Funnel Principle*. Over the past eighteen years, thousands of men and women in 120 sales teams around the world have been trained and coached in this system. Many of our early clients are still using *The Funnel Principle* today, ten or twelve years into the journey.

My sales training and coaching practice today focuses on front line sales managers because I am fascinated with what they do and consumed by helping them do it better. They're the heroes that make sales training succeed. Unfortunately sometimes they're the weak leaders that let sales training programs fail. How sales managers coach and lead their salespeople has a lasting impression. I focus on this core function for another reason; I give the clients that hire me and my partners a much better shot at impacting what matters to them—achieving sales results.

I wasn't instantly skilled at revealing to these manager clients of mine how and why their coaching was exceptional, average or lousy. I poured through my personal notes of 600 coaching conversations from roughly 2012-2018 and saw patterns emerge. The patterns led to insights and the insights led to developing frameworks for coaching that I've applied to thousands of sessions since. Every new discovery regarding coaching puts new mysteries in front of me that I'm determined to unravel. Still, I have much to learn.

I knew a poor coaching conversation when I heard one, but it took me a while to be able to deconstruct it and lead a conversation with the manager about what happened and why. What it really took was me getting out of my own way. You'll discover a lot more about my own personal journey shortly and how it helped me become not just a better executive coach to sales leaders, but also a better man.

My philosophies around sales coaching are a synthesis of influences that have challenged me to become a better person. These influences are not found in sales or business books but in books on personal transformation, vulnerability, psychology, spirituality, religion, personal growth, and the tragedies of falling and the beautiful recoveries that have followed. With the sales leader's role in mind, I have processed the insightful thinking of authors and professionals like Richard Rohr, Henry Cloud, Brene Brown, Bob Buford, Annie Lamott, Thomas Merton,

Henri Nouwen, Matthew Kelly, Fr. James Martin, Fr. Gregory Boyle, Joel Osteen, John Maxwell, Wayne Dyer, and John Wooden. These are the people that sales leaders should be reading about and learning from. This is my effort to bring that to you.

One thought-leader in selling I would like to recognize is Mike Bosworth. I attended a 3-day workshop that Mike led several years ago. I was surprised to hear him spend so much time on the topic of vulnerability. I had never associated vulnerability with selling, let alone with my life. Since then I gained great respect for what being more vulnerable can do for my relationships with people. Thanks Mike.

In summary, because of your blindspots, you're not achieving all that you are designed to achieve, even though you may think you're doing just fine. I hope my book sparks a fantastic transformation of your own.

To be clear, I'm not a research firm and I haven't done any studies per se on this topic. I don't make my living delivering snappy, charismatic speeches to crowded national sales meetings. I'm in the trenches with salespeople and sales managers one on one. What I write is 100% my opinion, based on what I've personally lived, experienced and witnessed. At times I'd have preferred some of the experiences to go away, but I now know they were gifts. Another gift is spending hours on the phone, year after year, hearing the interplay between sales managers and their salespeople. *Blindspots* is my way of processing those conversations with my personal experiences.

So how exactly will you benefit from this book? First, I am speaking directly to sales managers. You'll learn what blindspots are, why you have them, and how they lead to getting in your own way as you manage your salespeople. This awareness is a necessary first step. You'll discover your own blindspots and understand why they block you from greater coaching impact. Finally, you'll learn what you can do to reduce or even eliminate your blindspots. I can't guarantee any specific results, but I can tell you that my clients are getting measurable value, including:

- ✓ Getting more salespeople to hit quota
- ✓ Growing sales
- ✓ Selling more profitably
- ✓ Helping "B" players on the sales team become "A" players
- ✓ Accelerating the departure of low performers
- ✓ Having lower unforced turnover of the sales team
- ✓ Getting salespeople to have more loyalty to their managers and to embrace the responsibility of being on the team
- ✓ Getting more value from the CRM (customer relationship management) system as a tool for selling

You wouldn't be reading this if you weren't motivated to improve. I applaud you for that. This book might challenge you in unique ways and it might make you uncomfortable. Richard Rohr said that the truth will set you free, but at first it might make you miserable. You'll have to trust that getting uncomfortable is always necessary toward the next step in growth.

Part 1: The Vice in the Virtue

1

Your Blindspots Are Killing You – And Everyone Else

"Sometimes the hardest battle to win is the one you don't know you are fighting."
– Mark Sellers

If you are a sales manager looking for ways to be a more effective coach and leader of your salespeople, you've come to the right place. I can help you. But I warn you. Don't expect a book full of tips and techniques to memorize, shortcuts, or a top ten list of surefire ways to drive higher results. You'll need to uncover your blindspots, ways that you act and behave that are killing your coaching and leadership.

I want to take you beyond the tempting yet incomplete realm of 'how to' because this skips over a vital phase - understanding the root cause of your coaching and leadership gaps and the reasons your coaching and leadership has reached a plateau. By understanding the root cause of your blindspots you will grasp the underlying motives and influences that prevent you from becoming more fully the person, coach and sales leader you can be. You may have to go somewhere you may not have been; somewhere that traditional sales coaching has not taken you. You'll need to be vulnerable. You'll need to accept that you routinely get in your own way. You'll need to trust the process and path I'm taking you down. I can't guarantee you'll have the same transformative impact that I've had, but there's a good chance you'll experience growth like you've never realized. It can be that good.

Most of all, you have to learn to confront your blindspots, which is often difficult because sometimes they're hidden in the good stuff, making them hard to recognize. A vice in the virtue. For instance, too much passion can become an unbridled obsession, like a soccer mom or dad who forgets it's just a game. An ambitious drive to succeed, a virtue, can become an unhealthy desire, a vice.

If this is beginning to sound heavy, so be it. There's a lot at stake and there's a good chance you don't realize it.

Before I explain what a blindspot is, let me suggest that there's something generally accepted, fundamental, and even pivotal to your salespeople achieving quota year after year. They're more likely to hit that quota when they are motivated to sell for you, their sales manager. And they're more likely to be motivated if you make emotional connections with them. Let's connect some dots:

- **Motivated salespeople hit quota.**
- **Emotional connections create motivated salespeople.**

As it is with people in general you've probably found it easier to make an emotional connection with some salespeople. Your conversations with them seem to naturally flow. The coaching you give is more easily received. For these people you seem to know what to say and how to say it to get the response you want and and the outcome they need.

By contrast, you may have found that making an emotional

connection with other salespeople doesn't come effortlessly. Maybe these sellers repeat the same behaviors that you're constantly trying to break. This frustrates the hell out of you. It might drive you crazy. Instead of creating an emotional connection you're stressed out.

Salespeople respond favorably to having a sales manager for whom they are motivated to sell. They are eager to sell for a manager who has their back, determined to deliver results for a manager who motivates them. Even those who seem to want to be left alone deep down want more than just the commissions and the thrill of the hunt—they want their managers to stroke, coddle, praise, affirm, and lavish attention on them. They want recognition. Salespeople are willing to accept a tough message from managers like this. Let's connect another dot:

- **Motivated salespeople hit quota.**
- **Emotional connections create motivated salespeople.**
- **Salespeople want to sell for managers they are emotionally connected to.**

The problem is your blindspots are out to sabotage your ability to create emotional connections, build relationships with your salespeople, and motivate them to succeed.

So, what exactly is a blindspot?

Blindspots are behaviors you exhibit
that prevent you from making an emotional connection with the
people you lead and that negatively impact performance.

Think of blindspots like this: they are things you say that you shouldn't say to your people. They're things that you do that you shouldn't do to your people. They're the things that you should say that you don't say, and things that you should do that you don't do with your people. These behaviors are blindspots because you aren't aware that you do them.

Blindspots: The Hidden Killer of Sales Coaching

I've personally witnessed all kinds of blindspots including:

A vice president barged into a conference room occupied by me and her sales manager and said to the sales manager "You caused me to miss my number this quarter." I know this vice president well enough to know she cares deeply for the manager. But for that brief moment she didn't realize how her approach would not get her what she wanted. There are better ways to discuss the issue of not hitting a number.

Another vice president of another client came into a conference room where I was doing a coaching workshop for his two sales managers, introduced himself to me, but didn't ask me who I was, what we were doing and how it was going. Instead he turned to his managers and said "Have you seen our numbers this month? They're down and we need to get them up." He then walked out. In a way I wasn't surprised. The managers had shared with me earlier their struggles in working with their boss.

During a sales pipeline review I heard a sales rep tell his manager about finally getting in to see a hard to see prospect. The manager, instead of saying something like "that's great news!", paused for at least ten seconds and finally said, "Is it on your funnel?"

In each of these examples the managers commiting the blindspot behaviors are good people. They want their salespeople to do well. But their behaviors do not inspire, encourage or motivate. I'm convinced they are blind to how they reacted in these situations. They have blindspots.

Here are some common examples of blindspots:
- Talking over people or cutting them off
- Not paying attention to someone who is talking to you
- Not recognizing or celebrating someone's accomplishment
- Trying to fix someone's behavior that you think is flawed
- Exhibiting know-it-all behavior
- Not saying you're sorry

Your Blindspots Are Killing You – And Everyone Else

- Not admitting a mistake
- Passing judgment on someone
- Being prideful

Blindspots can also be behaviors that you are aware of doing but you just can't stop doing. For example, sometimes when my wife is speaking to me I get distracted. I know this about myself. Sometimes I catch myself immediately after doing it but it's too late - she lets me have it. I think this must run in my family because both my father and brother do this all the time and it drives me crazy. It is rude. It might not be fatal, but over time it sure does annoy people on the receiving end of it. Note to self: work harder on this blindspot.

Think of how annoying and distracting this kind of blindspot could have on a team of salespeople you lead. When one of your salespeople is talking to you he sure hopes you're giving him your undivided attention. How do you think he feels when he senses you're not? Email my wife, she can tell you.

Before the start of the 2018 college football season Ohio State head coach Urban Meyer unwittingly professed to his own blindspot regarding his program. Meyer was heavily criticized for not being 100% transparent with information he knew regarding an assistant coach. Meyer was also heavily criticized for not knowing more about this situation. The PR damage crushed Meyer, the football team and the university. Ohio State president Michael Drake suspended Meyer for the first three games of the season.

Why did coach Meyer think it could be OK to not be fully transparent? Why didn't he know more about the situation? Could it be his blindspots?

In the press conference the day before his first game back following the suspension, Meyer was asked if he thought that members of his staff were reluctant to bring him negative information. "I hope not", he said. People need to feel comfortable coming to me. I always thought I created that atmosphere." Well, maybe coach was wrong.

If you're a college football fan - even if you're not a fan of the Buckeyes! - you know that Urban Meyer strikes a serious and intimidating demeanor. Would you like to bring him bad news? His blindspot was in not seeing that his serious, intimidating demeanor might actually create the opposite of what he wanted - instead of people feeling comfortable coming to him with negative information he encouraged them not to.

I know people who personally know coach Meyer. I have every reason to believe that he is a good man who cares deeply about his players and coaches and his community. The expectations of a public figure like coach are reasonably high, easily matched by the public's appetite for castigating perceived missteps.

Is it possible that how you think you come across to the people you lead is different from how you actually come across? In fact, how fully aware can you be of how you come across to anyone? There's really only one way to know. You need a high level of self-awareness. This requires a healthy amount of humility and vulnerability, and you get that mostly by working on it. Most people don't. Leaders especially have many competing interests to high self-awareness, mostly traceable to ego. So give yourself a break, but also let's get to work!

Another blindspot involves a person we might call a know-it-all. Have you ever seen an interview with the U.S. Senator Rand Paul? He's a smart guy, a doctor and he comes across as a know-it-all. This is unflattering and doesn't endear him to people. Bill Maher is also a smart, entertaining guy who comes across as a know it all. I've watched Maher zone off when guests are talking. He looks like he doesn't have the patience to listen any more. It's hard to emotionally connect with someone that treats people like this.

The know-it-all's blindspot is thinking that having all of the answers is all that matters. They seem almost allergic to the idea of asking genuine questions, not the type they ask when they already know the answer. These people tell but don't ask. A sales manager know-it-all doesn't realize that her telling isn't coaching, her answers aren't what her salespeople need. To coach and lead better these managers have to have this questioning capability arrow in their quivers.

I told a client of mine about this kind of blindspot. She said she could relate. Earlier in her career when she was promoted she was told that while she was smart, capable, and ambitious and would likely go far she could sometimes come across a bit arrogant, and that she would become a better leader if she learned to dial this back. She had no idea what he was talking about. She was just being herself. It's not easy to change something like this because it's related to how she's wired. Instead of shrinking, however, from the constructive criticism, she devoted herself to changing. I don't know her 'before' but I do know her 'after' and my experience coaching her has been tremendously satisfying. She asks lots of questions. She's curious. She seeks coaching. In my book she's a rock star.

Blindspots between spouses are common. My wife has a habit of creating piles of stuff scattered throughout the house. It could be anything such as mail, a shopping bag whose contents are scattered on the kitchen table, shoes, keys, trinkets, whatever. For years I chose to let this really bother me and made it my project to 'fix her', not an endearing emotion. After 30 years of marriage I've finally chosen to not let this bother me as much and as such my tension and judgment do not drain the oxygen from every room I enter.

Some blindspots can seem somewhat harmless, but they have the same effect that potholes have on cars—hitting one once a year may rattle your teeth but hitting one once a week for years and you're likely headed to the local repair shop.

Blindspots: The Hidden Killer of Sales Coaching

So how do you begin to eliminate or dial back your blindspots? You have to embrace a paradox that is difficult for everyone I've ever worked with. You know about paradoxes. A few of my favorites are 'nothing succeeds like failure', and 'nothing fails like success'. Churchill said "If I had more time I would have written a shorter letter." All of these are counterintuitive. All of these are true.

Most of us can relate to the paradox of something physical like getting in shape or improving a 10K time. We need to feel pain to feel better. But to be a better coach and leader what's the necessary pain and paradox?

Try this exercise to find out:

On a sheet of paper write down three traits or characteristics of yourself that you know have had a big impact on your professional and personal success. Think of not only your present day success, like the job you have but also think of your childhood successes. Maybe you excelled in sports or academics. Maybe you started a business. Maybe you were an eagle scout.

Got your three traits? Here's the paradox.

These traits will someday betray you. It's likely already happened. If you don't think so, you've just discovered a blindspot. To be clear, these traits will cause you pain, struggles, and suffering. No one is immune to it.

This can be confusing. Let me tell you how my three traits betrayed me.

I claim discipline, ambition and ability to sacrifice as three traits instrumental to my success. They helped me jump my mother's car on my bicycle when I was 13 years old. They helped me be a two-time conference champion golfer of the year in high school. They helped me play golf in college. They helped me write two books and start and grow two companies. I taught myself to play the guitar. I ran two marathons, one in under three and a half hours. They helped me provide a lot of things like opportunities, material possessions, vacations, experiences, and more for my three kids and my wife. All of this took a lot of discipline, ambition and sacrifice.

So how did they betray me?

My sacrifice came at the cost of having no close friends and actually thinking I didn't need friends, up until several years ago. I convinced myself that friends took too much time and got in the way of what I was trying to achieve. I'm all for sacrifice to achieve things, but when it goes too far the virtue has become a vice.

My ambitions made me destructively selfish. I compared my success to those of others and felt like I was always in competition. I looked at everyone as a target to get what I wanted. I had selfish agendas. I'm sure at times I wasn't much fun to be around.

My discipline misled me. Because I was so capable of starting and finishing things on my own I didn't seek help or guidance. Isolation came easy. I convinced myself I needed it to constantly develop strategies and vision and direction for the business. I relied on no one. Discipline also made me an unloving drill sergeant at home. I thought being a good parent was defining rules, driving expectations, and correcting people when they tripped up.

Fortunately I've changed in dramatic ways. My journey started about seven years ago on a business trip to Singapore that lead to discovering a serious blindspot. You will learn about this in the next chapter.

I hope you can begin to see how your blindspots connect directly to leadership and coaching. The inability to embrace the vice in the virtue paradox (eg ambition is healthy but unbridled ambition can be unhealthy) keeps you locked into a comfort zone that deprives you of greater impact on people. We are trapped in that comfort zone because we have a tendency to double down on the traits that made us successful - could we be blamed? We have the track record to show for it. The problem is we don't grow. Your blindspots prevent you from seeing that the people you lead might not have the same success traits as you. And therefore you can't see that how someone with your traits wants to be coached and be led is not the same as how someone with different success traits needs to be coached and be led.

Here's another exercise. Think of someone who is not like you, who doesn't share your top three traits. Is it one of your kids? Is it one of your parents or a sibling? Is it your spouse? Is it a salesperson you manage? Have you ever become totally frustrated with this person's inability to do something you have asked him or her to do, something that you have done hundreds of times? How did you react? Did your blindspot get the best of you?

If it did you probably didn't create an emotional connection, and you probably didn't get what you wanted.

> **Remember, while your blindspots are things you can't see, they are usually in plain view of everyone else.**

To summarize, the challenge of dealing with your blindspots comes down to a paradox. The things that cause your blindspots are also the things that have helped you survive and succeed. It's the vice in the virtue. But the way out is the way through. I've never seen it be easy. You'll have to unravel the meaning in that paradox yourself, but ironically, you'll need the help of others. Including me. Let's connect some more dots.

- **Motivated salespeople hit quota.**
- **Emotional connections create motivated salespeople.**
- **Salespeople want to sell for managers they are emotionally**

connected to.

- **Blindspots prevent emotional connections.**

In part 1 you'll learn that you have these blindspots and you get in your own way. You'll learn that blindspots come from how you are wired, fundamentally your personality. This is something you had no control over. But don't think you can't still change even if you can't re-wire yourself. I can tell you from personal experience and that of my clients that if you are intentional about your blindspots not only will you coach better, you'll be a better person with everyone you meet in your life.

In Part 2 you'll learn how blindspots are also due to an obsession for and transparency of sales data. Another paradox. More data is supposed to make you smarter but it doesn't necessarily make you coach and lead better. The incredible amount of data most organizations now have, combined with unprecedented visibility and transparency of all that data creates a blindspot for sales managers.

Finally in Part 3 I suggest that your company's sales processes could actually be an obstacle to creating emotional connections and doing what you intend them to do for you — have better coaching conversations. Another paradox.

I close by suggesting that ongoing coaching can help you deal with blindspots and give you a lifetime of benefits that impact everyone you encounter.

So let's get on with it. Let's learn why you get in your own way.

2

Getting in Your Own Way

"Awareness is curative."
– Surya Das

Blindspots come in all shapes and sizes and they often cause us to get in our own way. Blindspots are behaviors that are usually obvious to everyone but that are hidden to us. These aren't one-time isolated events. They're patterns of repeated behavior. They are our familiar roads and well worn grooves and we've convinced ourselves of their virtue. We don't see the vice, until it's too late.

We see this played out in public all the time with famous people—the Hollywood star who crashes and burns from drug or alcohol addiction; the political lobbyist who pushes the limits too far and is finally indicted; the boxer who didn't know when to retire the gloves. Though you probably don't live a famous life, you get in your own way every bit as much as famous people and you suffer your own consequences that become part of your daily battles.

One example of a public figure and his blindspots is Frasier Crane in the long running, highly successful sitcom *Frasier*. Eighteen years after the final "Goodnight Seattle" episode, it is still one of my wife's favorite television shows, guaranteed to make her laugh. She summed up the essence of the sitcom by saying that deep down Frasier was eternally searching for love, but when it repeatedly arrived he couldn't get himself to surrender to it. This failure to surrender is a root cause of blindspots.

Frasier was a hostage to the things he coveted much more than the things that deep down would bring him far greater fulfillment, like love. He coveted his gorgeous Seattle condominium and its iconic skyline (could you blame him?) and his status in his professional and personal communities. He also coveted control. Fittingly, many of the hilarious moments resulted from his control backfiring on him. What would otherwise be good fodder for a tragic drama was masterfully used to make us all laugh.

Frasier consistently got in his own way. Like all of us, Frasier had serious blindspots. He committed unforced errors all the time, misguided by his outsized ego. A humbler, less self-centered Frasier would have lived a more fulfilling life. But then who would tune in to watch that?

The superb show, *The Crown*, has another example of someone getting in his own way. At the end of his legendary career, Winston Churchill is depicted as not knowing it was time to resign as prime minister and let the new leaders take the reins of Great Britain's future. In one episode the portraitist Graham Sutherland is commissioned by Parliament to paint Churchill's official painting. It's a hint from party leaders that it's time to move on and it doesn't escape Churchill. He is 80 years old, always hunched over, and in declining health. Yet he desperately clings to his image as leader.

When he sees Sutherland's painting the first time, in private, he is physically revolted and tells the artist he feels betrayed. The problem he has with the painting cuts to the brutal truth—it's too honest for Churchill's liking. In fact, throughout the painting process which took place over several sittings and months, he cautions Sutherland to choose historical dignity over honesty. "Remember, you're painting the office of the prime minister," he says. The scene where Churchill sees the painting for the first time reaches a climax when Churchill yells, "It is cruel!" And the painter yells back, "Age is cruel! If you see decay, that's because there is decay...if you see frailty, that's because there's frailty." Finally, the artist says, "If you're engaged in a fight with something, it's not me; it's your own blindness."

Later, when Churchill is alone, emotionally exhausted from the reflection, he comes to a realization and says, "I am that man in the painting, wretched and decaying." He resigns shortly after.

What was so obvious to everyone else was so hidden and unimaginable to Churchill. A big blindspot.

We Need to Get Personal

Later, we'll look at how outside forces such as data can create blindspots, but here we need to get personal. I will help you see that most of your blindspots are rooted in your very own, very personal make up, the DNA so to speak of who you are.

Blindspots cause you to get in your own way and delving into their roots may not be comfortable, like hearing the sound of your voice played back to you for the first time.

To uncover your blindspots, you'll have to unpack your story and you may not be flattered by what you find. But if you allow yourself to go there, you're well on your way to incredibly meaningful discovery and possible breakthroughs that will reveal a lot about how well you emotionally connect with your salespeople and everyone else.

Getting in Your Own Way – Mark's Blindspot

I can write about this topic because I have lots of practice getting in my own way. Since it's asking a lot of you to personally reflect, I'll go first. I want to share with you two big blindspots I had several years ago.

The First Blindspot

I started my sales training business twenty three years ago by becoming an independent franchisee for a well known global sales training company. Ten years into that relationship my restlessness and curiosity about sales training and methods led me to leave to form a new sales training business and launch a sales model I created called The BuyCycle Funnel™ and a selling system called The Funnel Principle. I published a book by the same name in 2008. Today The Funnel Principle selling system has been implemented by 120 sales teams in 27 countries around the world. We'll take a deep dive into it in Chapter 6.

A key part of the Funnel Principle system is the Funnel Audit™, a monthly 1:1, 45- to 60-minute structured coaching conversation between a sales manager and his or her salesperson about the health of the salesperson's funnel. Companies hire me to listen to these Funnel Audit conversations via conference call and then coach the managers on what I heard. The sales managers, not the salespeople, are the focus of my coaching.

My intent, no surprise, was to help the sales managers get competent in having a Funnel Audit conversation. I was good at doing this. Then, after several years I found myself hearing things on these calls that I hadn't heard before because I hadn't been listening for these things before. I was hearing *the tone of the conversations,* like the tension or excitement in the sales manager's voice; I was hearing the anxiety or frustration in a salesperson's reply to a manager's questions, as if he felt that the questions were an interrogation; I heard the elation when a breakthrough was made; I heard the exasperation when the manager couldn't get some important point across; I heard tension in the salesperson's replies that sometimes suggested he was tired of the call and wanted to hang up. Many times the calls were so intense or ineffectively breaking down I wanted to ring the bell to declare the end of the round. But some conversations were so productive and a delight to listen to. Anyone listening could tell that good coaching took place.

I became increasingly intrigued by my newfound awareness. What good was it if a sales manager could technically work through the Funnel Audit but could not emotionally connect with the salesperson and inspire greater performance? I felt that I was onto something insightful that could improve my clients' coaching, but I didn't yet have clarity. I continued to study why some coaching conversations were great while others were poor. And then, it hit me. This was a blindspot I had for many years:

Within the *virtue* of the Funnel Audit conversation was also the *vice*. The virtue of the Audit was in how it transformed how sales managers *could* communicate with sellers around funnel health and sales opportunities. The vice of the Audit was how it could create an environment *that suppressed that communication* and denied the manager and salesperson all of the benefits of it.

A paradox. You can't get the virtue of the Audit without exposing yourself to the vice of the Audit. It became clearer. The virtue was easier to see because I focused on seeing it. The vice was trickier to understand because it was hidden by the virtue.

All of this was trying to teach me that I should shift my coaching attention away from the mechanics of the Funnel Audit and instead to the whole person, the sales manager. The manager needed more than just a coach to advise on an Audit conversation; she needed advice on how to make an impact with her salespeople, how to truly connect and motivate and inspire.

This stressed me because I was not sure I could make this shift. What qualified me to get personal with sales managers? Why would they consider me credible in discussing things not Audit related? Could I learn to put my attention on the whole person and not just the Audit conversation? Could I coach on how to inspire and motivate?

To do this I needed to make major changes. I needed to learn to listen better and differently during the Audit conversations. I needed to understand human behavior better. I needed to know how to develop deeper trust with the managers so that they would respect my feedback about their behaviors.

Eventually I committed to making this pivot in my business, but in truth, I wasn't equipped to deliver dramatically different coaching just yet. Fortunately, however, I had another blindspot brewing that was the key to filling that gap. This second blindspot, much more personal than the first one, helped me gain the perspective I needed to help my clients and myself in ways that would impact personal and professional lives.

The Second Blindspot

Soon after publishing *The Funnel Principle*, I became quite popular as a speaker, trainer and consultant, thanks to a partnership with my dear friend Gerhard Gschwandtner, publisher of *Selling Power* magazine. For several years I sponsored many of his Sales 2.0 and Leadership conferences where I found my leads and my clients found me.

I was very busy and traveling a lot, often internationally. It was nothing for me to be gone several days in a row every week for several weeks. My wife held down the house with our two teenage girls, Hannah and Polly, and our youngest, our son Patrick.

Besides the stress that being gone creates for an active young family, to make matters worse, when I was home I wasn't really 'there.' I always had so much prep to do for client work or a speaking engagement. Or I was always working on the next deal. I spent a lot of time in my home office or I'd be thinking about work all the time. If you would've asked me then how I felt about this lifestyle, I would have told you that yes it was stressful for everyone but that following my passion, taking risks, and working my ass off was God's blessing for me. I was a role model to my kids. Work hard, set goals, and get what you want. All the sacrifice? It's just the price anyone has to pay to be successful.

The truth was I was so single-minded in my ambition I couldn't see the selfishness right in front of me.

Singapore

I ran hard for several years. A pivotal moment occurred on a business trip to Singapore in 2012. I returned to my hotel room after a client dinner. I pulled back the drapes to see the stunning view of the Marina Bay in beautiful downtown Singapore. I saw the iconic Marina Bay Sands Casino and the Arts/Science Museum which is shaped like a lotus flower. I marveled at the lights of all of the buildings sparkling against the jet black southeast Asia sky.

As a sales trainer and coach I was at the top of my game. Five years earlier I published The Funnel Principle. It was named a top ten best book to read by Selling Power magazine. I was a thought leader. Gerhard Gschwandtner called it 'revolutionary'. I had the recognition of peers. I had marquis clients. I was traveling all over the world. I was impressed with myself.

I shut the drapes, went to the edge of my bed, sat down and wept like a child.

In reality I was a wreck inside and didn't know it. My success felt empty. My accomplishments seemed insignificant. What the hell was wrong with me? This was crazy! I was doing exactly what I envisioned and worked so hard to achieve. Over the next few weeks I tried to forget and deny what happened but it wouldn't let go of me. Over the next several months I had recurring episodes of what I experienced in Singapore. I was a long way from knowing what I know now - that this episode was the necessary painful spark that exposed a serious blindspot.

What exactly was my blindspot? The vision I created of myself didn't match who I really was. That's not to say I shouldn't be a sales trainer or executive coach, or that I shouldn't write books or travel when necessary, or that I shouldn't have marquis clients. I am good at the work and it fulfills me. I had let my ego take control of defining me and that lead to taking a certain path that was not the best version of myself. In short, I became self-absorbed and driven to serve me first. Other than that I was a pretty good guy! The ego is too self-obsessed to trust with your destiny. While it helped me succeed in some impressive ways it also prevented me from succeeding in other, more fulfilling ways. The vices in my virtues lead to a serious imbalance.

I had no idea yet about vices in virtues and the gift of the paradox but I got to work on me. Shortly after, a close friend, Steve, mysteriously showed up with some spiritual books that helped me learn the questions I should be asking. He had no idea what I was going through. Why did he decide to lend me these books then? I began, on my own, to unpack my story. How did I really get here? Where was 'here'?

One epiphany early on was realizing that I was not a 'self-made' man. No one is a self-made man. Each of us is the product of our relationships. When I realized that, I stopped taking so much credit for what I had accomplished. I asked myself 'what was I afraid of happening if I took the focus off of me?' I asked 'what do I covet that I might need to give up?' I didn't want to give up anything, especially since I believed that what I coveted were the spoils of my well-deserved victories.

Blindspots: The Hidden Killer of Sales Coaching

Eventually as I took inventory of my life I saw something that I had never seen before. There was something present every step of the way with all of the things I accomplished - the traits that helped me succeed were also the traits that caused me pain, struggles and suffering. My virtues were my vices. I deceived myself into thinking that what I had accomplished was what defined me. And that the things I pursued to achieve I did primarily to define me. Being a published author, a thought leader, a speaker, having clients all over the world, these things defined me. I was very much into appearance. I fed off of the recognition and the association with other well-known thought leaders. I built a big house. I sent my kids to private schools. I lived a million dollar lifestyle. I wanted people to see that I was successful.

Starting the Journey

This opened my eyes. Where I thought I was passionate (healthy), deep down I was too intense and a workaholic (unhealthy). Where I thought I was living my dream (go for it!), leveraging the gifts God gave me (purpose), deep down I was selfish and conceited (feeding my ego).

It's important to realize that my belief in me and my ideas regarding sales was authentic. I loved the work. I loved my clients. My passion was genuine. I feared mostly letting a client down so I worked tirelessly to avoid that. I was grateful for their confidence and trust in me. I felt I brought important ideas to the profession. I had to find a different way to channel my gifts.

I began a painful, necessary journey back to finding the real me. I needed to let a part of me die so I sold the million dollar house my wife and I meticulously designed and loved (and coveted). We downsized to something that was more me and us. I loosened the rigidity around the house that stifled and smothered and kept my family at a distance. I started to put value on things I had previously considered less important.

More quality time with family. Service in my community. I joined the Knights of Columbus to commit to volunteering. I made time for friends.

I said yes to an invitation to attend my church's annual men's retreat. I witnessed men give talks about their personal struggles and challenges. I got more involved with this group. Two years later I was asked to be the emcee for one of these. The ultimate irony - the greatest honor I've ever been given and it's something I never strived for. I could feel my old skin peeling away and a new one replace it. I became a dad, husband, friend, son, and brother that people wanted to be around and get to know. A man less focused on himself and more genuinely interested in others.

This man was inside me the entire time. It took a serious emotional fall, humble reflection, and a conscious recovery to let him out.

Still Charging Hard, But with a Different Outlook

I've told my story a lot. Sometimes people interpret my story as simply a guy who needed to reduce his workload and recharge. Maybe reset some priorities. It can look like that, but it's much deeper.

To that point, my business is busier than ever. But now instead of boasting about my airline status I'm embarrassed to admit it. Instead of relishing being on the road, I see it as a necessary sacrifice. Instead of being unsettled at home and not present I really enjoy things like the goofiness of my two dogs, or doing a home project my wife gives me. The weeds in the flower beds, the laundry overflowing in the hallway, the dishes in the sink don't bother me like they used to.

Humility in the Form of Breakthrough

I've become a big fan of the power of humility. It was key to my transformation and unlocking that mysterious door that was the obstacle to me learning how I was getting in my own way. It unlocked that mystery of the vice inside the virtue, which is a theme of many breakthroughs and transformations in personal lives.

The very thing that you believe has gotten you where you are (virtue), that you have worked so hard to master, that you rightfully claim as your strengths, and that you fight to defend every day as key to your success is the very thing that now blocks you from getting better (vice). You're stuck and you don't know why. This is a blindspot. It's an intense contradiction. It's similar to the axiom that you only get what you want when you stop wanting it so badly. How could something that has been so necessary to you, your virtue, suddenly be a vice, a major block to your continued growth?

The Gift of Falling

When you consider the price you have to pay to see the vice in the virtue, it's no wonder we often don't discover it. That's because it usually takes falling before you can rise. My fall in Singapore was necessary for me to grow. And when we fall and accept it, instead of fighting it, we can begin to let the part of us die that needs to die. The selfishness that fueled personal ambition must die to make room for a flood of generosity and unconditional love that comes from being unselfish. The control that assured individual attainment must die to make room for the unexpected treasures that new trust and faith will bring.

There are countless examples of men and women falling and dying that we can learn from. Scott Harrison fell and founded Charity: Water, an organization that provides clean drinking water to millions of people. Saint Augustine gave up a coveted, selfish, career as a teacher of rhetoric in Milan to become one of the most influential writers of early Christian doctrine. Michael Phelps fell hard—battling drug and alcohol abuse—after what must have been a suffocating, sacrificing life of devoting every grain of his existence to winning 23 gold medals. A good friend of mine left a high-powered, high-paying job in business to rescue his family from the effects that his stressful career had on everyone around him. He's happier now and at peace teaching math to high schoolers and being deeply involved in his faith community.

We sometimes don't see the vice in the virtue because we tend to have a dualistic perspective on life. We prefer black or white, left or right, republican or democrat, etc. We don't like gray. We like buckets and categories. We define things that we align with as much by defining what we don't align with. We don't like enemies but deep down we need them to define who we claim we're not. This dualistic mindset locks us into patterns and habits that block growth and contribute to feeding our selfish interests. It prevents us from seeing the vice in the virtue.

When you explore the contradiction instead of just choosing sides, you're taking a courageous first step in admitting to yourself that something you've considered a virtue or a strength may now be a vice. This will be incredibly confusing at first. And unfortunately, it usually gets worse before it gets better, and it's humbling. You might not be ready for that level of vulnerability, which will keep you imprisoned in your own selfishness. You've got to sort of unwind what you've wound so tightly.

Even when you've become aware of a blindspot there's no guarantee this awareness will change your life, because you're more than likely to ignore it or deny it and hope it never reappears. These are tough choices. Our church holds an offsite, one-day men's retreat for men who have never been on a men's retreat. It's often hard to get guys to sign up. On the surface it seems like it's life's busyness that competes and prevents them from attending. But it's more about their hesitation to be vulnerable and expose themselves to some demons. I don't mean to pass judgment. I was that guy for years who said no. My friend John asked me every year to attend for several years. I was always too busy.

So now that we've looked at a couple of my blindspots, let's go searching for some of yours.

Types of Sales Managers

Your management style could reveal some of your blindspots. Read the profiles below and be honest with yourself. Better yet, ask someone who knows you to read them and tell you what they think. Don't be too hard on yourself. I hope you find a little humor in this as well as insight. Finally, you may find that you have characteristics of more than one profile.

The Activity Cop: The activity cop sales manager is obsessed with completing tasks. She loves the checklist. She appears less interested in helping her salespeople get things done and more interested in pointing out what's not yet complete. She's an awesome compliance officer, but often not a very good coach.

Activity cops can put salespeople on edge. These managers sometimes interpret this edge as a positive motivator. It's not. The blindspot for activity cops is not seeing how their insistent rigidity on completing tasks becomes the distracting focus of conversations. For example, a salesperson who needs a lot of affirmation will recoil when an activity cop obsesses about what's not yet done.

One of the blindspots for activity cops is treating all tasks as equally important. A checkbox is a checkbox to her instead of prioritizing tasks that are most important.

It's tempting to want to applaud the person who wants to get things done, but the activity cop manager has taken the virtue too far. It's now become a vice.

The Process Preacher: The process preacher sees his job as making sure people *follow the rules*. He believes that sales success is found through processes, systems and policies and cannot be achieved any other way. He can be extremely rigid and inflexible to a fault. He often has little capacity to consider an alternative point of view.

One of the process preacher's blindspots is confusing bureaucracy with sales process. The latter can be powerful, and the former can be insufferable. A set of steps to follow doesn't constitute a process and it doesn't mean the steps make the person more productive.

Another blindspot for process preachers is in thinking that the only way to achieve sales objectives, such as quota, is through the company's defined sales process. That's not true. Many top sellers have unique ways of doing their jobs outside of any corporate process. A process preacher can alienate a top producing salesperson who has his own way of selling that's not in line with a corporate process. This manager can struggle to lead and motivate these reps.

While sales managers need to show everyone on their team where to find the value in the sales process, top salespeople will challenge them the most since they're most likely the ones who resist changes in the way they sell.

The Know-It-All Sales Manager: Know-it-all sales managers lead their sales teams by a simple creed. They know what's best. They believe they are always right, and being right is a virtue *above all else*. They have probably fought their whole lives to be right. This is a big burden for anyone to carry.

There can be several blindspots for a know-it-all sales manager. One, she struggles to make emotional connections with her salespeople and therefore doesn't have as much of an impact. Her people might not feel like "taking the hill" for these managers.

Two, a know-it-all manager craves the spotlight and recognition to be seen as right. Therefore, she doesn't easily give recognition if it takes away from her own.

Three, the know-it-all manager might struggle to coach because she doesn't have the patience for letting her salespeople learn. Learning takes time. It often takes failing. Instead of putting up with that, the know-it-all manager could be doing something else. Her coaching is mostly telling rather than listening and communicating.

Four, because no one gets it like the know-it-all manager does, her reaction to salespeople that don't get it can be very critical. Persistent criticism can wear salespeople down and clip their motivations. It's common for know-it-all managers to come across as judgmental.

Salespeople might shut down with these managers and put up a defense to protect themselves, leaving them less likely to seek coaching.

The Title Defender: The title defender is a manager who believes the title makes the person instead of the person making the title. A classic title defender is the father who sets rules for the house and makes it clear that the only reason he needs for setting the rules is that he is the father of the house. These types of fathers or mothers can have high compliance commitment. They can also raise resentful children who aren't eager to get together any time soon after leaving.

The title defender knows the title gives him a certain position over his salespeople but confuses that position with earned respect. Sometimes he is respected less. His blindspot is in not seeing that his perception of the title status prevents him from creating a connection with his salespeople.

The title defender might aspire to the job largely because he longs for the status and position that he believes the title gives him. Nothing wrong with ambition but without purpose, title defenders might be hard pressed to be effective leaders of salespeople.

The Super Salesman Manager: The Super Salesman Manager is a salesperson disguised as a sales manager. He defines his importance and value by his direct actions in selling, instead of by how well his salespeople sell and grow and develop. He finds ways to insert himself into sales calls he makes with his salespeople. He jumps in and justifies this action by "preventing the call going badly" and "making sure an opportunity is seized." He believes he serves the company best this way. He tends to coach by telling, and he expects the salesperson to watch and learn how he does things and then be able to assimilate.

He prefers the comfort of having control than the discomfort of letting his salespeople get dirty and learn. He might even be embarrassed by his sellers' actions and take it as a reflection of him.

The blindspot is that he doesn't see this behavior comes at the cost of developing his salespeople. His salespeople can feel defensive or nervous around the super salesman manager. They can lose their respect for these managers. They can reach a point where they no longer trust the manager.

The Laptop Leader: The Laptop Leader is a sales manager who manages mostly from her office instead of spending time in the field with her people. She might be great with data, dashboards and excel spreadsheets, maybe even more comfortable with data than with people. The problem with the Laptop Leader is that her people are denied the value of many things like the simple camaraderie of working together, watching the manager lead an important meeting, or sharing frustrations or celebrating a win.

These managers lose touch with their salespeople and they might also lose touch with their customers.

The blindspots for a laptop leader are not seeing the impact that her lack of physical presence has with her people. She can also have blindspots for thinking that the data tell the whole story about her salespeople.

Blindspots: The Hidden Killer of Sales Coaching

The Do-It-Like-Me Manager: This sales manager sees himself as a great model of how to be successful in the sales job. Often, he was successful as a salesperson and he believes strongly in the path to success that he took.

Sometimes the Do-It-Like-Me Manager had to figure out on his own how to do the sales job and be successful. Maybe his company provided no formal training or personal development. It's often impressive what he's done with no guidance, but unfortunately, he may have no independent benchmark for how to do the job. He might even be cynical or skeptical of training methods for selling.

A blindspot with the Do-It-Like-Me Managers is that they assume everyone should approach the sales job the way they did. Of course, when these managers have salespeople who are wired like them then this style could work.

But what works for one salesperson might not work entirely for another one. Philosophies could be different. Maybe the market or territory has changed over the years. There's actually little coaching going on if the manager forces each salesperson into his sales success template. There's more likely to be a lot of telling and talking instead of communicating.

Another blindspot comes with hiring. If a Do-It-Like-Me Manager hires people who are a lot like him, then he won't grow as much and develop new skills by which to manage and lead.

Breakthrough

It's easy to be blind to the behaviors in you that negatively affect the people you interact with. They're blindspots. Awareness is the first step. Then you have to learn to get out of your own way.

Why do we get in our own way? Let's find out.

3

Why You Get in Your Own Way

"The you that you think is you is not you, it's your ego."
– Jordan Peterson, author of *The 12 Rules for Life*:
An Antidote to Chaos

"The ego is the hustler and the message is, 'hustle for your worth.'"
– Brené Brown, author of five #1 *New York Times*
bestsellers, leading expert on
vulnerability

Before we jump into helping you get out of your own way, you need to know why you get in your own way in the first place. The simple reason is that we are flawed. You might say we know better but why then do we act counter to what we know? In this chapter you'll learn that your blindspots are often fueled by ego that, in a way, has outlived its usefulness.

Ego is a very complicated thing. I'm not an expert on it but I do have my experiences to share. And there are many excellent books that analyze ego and its influences, some of which are listed in the appendix of this book. Fortunately, too, you don't need a PhD in psychology or counseling to relate with the information and perspectives of these resources and spark some changes in your life.

Blindspots: The Hidden Killer of Sales Coaching

Ego

The ego is defined by most dictionaries as *a person's sense of self-esteem or self-importance.* Right away you see that it's both critical to identification and it is "self- reporting." It's how you see you. Not surprisingly, there's likely a lot of room for error.

Ego probably is known more for its negative connotation than for anything positive. "He's got a big ego" isn't a flattering comment. But if ego is about identification of who you are, why can't ego just as easily drive a person to be more humble and less selfish, or more serving than self-serving? It can, and it's often a complex journey that starts with taking care of self that shifts to focusing less on self. Instead of looking at ego as bad or good, which is a limiting dualistic and insufficient view, and one that won't help you with your shadow boxing and inner work to become a better sales leader, think of ego as a sort of command center that develops as you live and mature. It plays an important role in how you respond to your world and how you claim your place in it. Claiming your place isn't a one-time event, but rather a life-long journey as you move along the road to maturity.

Ego and the Arc of Life

Let's think of ego in relation to the arc of your life. If you're fortunate to live long enough, you go through several major phases. These phases don't necessarily have hard and fast boundaries but they are distinct enough from each other. Also, it's not as though everyone moves through the phases in a super clean, linear and chronological fashion. Some younger people have had life experiences that make them wise beyond their years, and some older people still behave like children. But for the most part envision yourself moving through these phases as you age.

First you are created. Before you know it your personality is developing. Ego is pulsating with every heartbeat. When I think of my three kids as infants I can vividly recall the differences in their personalities. With two now grown and on their own and one in high school, I won't attempt to even briefly describe them here for fear of any one of them taking offense with my description!

In the next phase you leave infancy behind and start to explore your world, and **ego is there shaping and being shaped by your experiences**. Your senses are alive with curiosity. You touch everything you can reach, you put things in your mouth, you walk and bump into things and fall down, and you hear and smell. Eventually you become aware of your physical and gender identity. Boys discover being boys and girls discover being girls, physically and emotionally. Your gender helps you process what you experience. The ego is developing with every experience—school, friendship, sibling dynamics, athletics, competition, parental and other family influences, birth order, the community you live in, hobbies, the music your parents listen to, or don't listen to, and more. Ego is vital for boys to become men and for girls to become women.

As you move through adolescence your ego is well on its way to being a mold that's rigidly cast. Whether you like it or not, by the time you're an early teen your personality is firmly defined.

Then you enter a phase where you learn to survive, mostly by fighting or competing. I'm not talking about physical fighting, though that can be a manifestation. I'm talking about emotional fighting. As a Type 3 on the Enneagram, a personality model, I relate to this idea of fighting and surviving. For some reason, when I was young I felt like the world was against me. I fought everything all the time. I got into fist fights at recess. I misbehaved throughout elementary school. Eventually, I channeled my anger into competing at baseball, basketball, and then golf. And I hated to lose. I always had something to prove. You'd want me on your team but I'm not sure you'd want to hang out with me.

In college, I fought to earn a spot on the golf team as a walk-on. Later I fought to win sales and achieve quotas. When I got laid off, which was the fortunate spark that eventually led me to formally start my training and coaching business, I fought to figure out what I should do with my life. In a way every year I fight to make it thrive. Writing books meant fighting through a lack of sleep to write early in the morning so I wouldn't interrupt my day job or take time away from raising three kids. When I look back on the past 23 years of this wonderful business and see what I've accomplished, I know it's because I'm a fighter. It doesn't make me any better than anyone else. It's all part of my journey and my arc of life.

This survival phase can begin very early in your life—maybe you know someone who grew up with either abusive parents or alcoholic parents and as a child had to grow up fast. They learned to survive in that home. For other people, the fighting phase can extend well into their senior years. These people tend to be closed minded, maybe not worldly or educated. They are set in their ways. Some people never escape from this phase.

Having this fighting mentality early on is healthy when fighting means surviving, so be sure to thank your ego for that. We just added a new dog to our family, a rescue Chihuahua named Louie. He was likely abused and suffered in some ways, which means he's even more of a piece of work. When he eats, he eats so fast it's like he's in a race. It makes me wonder if he didn't get fed much when he was young and had to fight for scraps at dinner time.

So ego helps you be a fighter and that's positive as you grow and develop. The problem is we tend to cling to ego far longer than we should. There comes a time in our lives when we don't need to fight so much for us; rather, we need to replace some of the fight with more compassion and forgiveness. We've all seen—or worse exhibited—ugly, ego-driven behavior. It's the soccer mom or dad behaving like a child on the side of the field, screaming at the refs, the players, and even the coaches. It's the public personalities who abuse their power and positions, like Matt Lauer or like Tiger Woods did. It's Rita Crundwell, the city manager for the small city of Dixon, Illinois, who embezzled $53M from her city to feed a lifestyle that was driven by a selfish ego beyond imagination. She lost all sense of reality.

It's Elizabeth Holmes, the former young, rising business star CEO of Theranos, who led a massive fraud scheme that fooled her board, investors, and the public and resulted in Theranos going from the mountain top to depths of the valley, bankrupt and shamed. Though Theranos machines never worked as claimed, Holmes presented a relentless face of confidence that things were on track and her "passion" and determination would lead the company to success. She never admitted she was or could be wrong and what she was doing was illegal.

It's rare that someone admits that he or she is wrong and you are right. In a training workshop with a client recently, one of the salesmen recounted a business owner he had been trying to sell a hot water system to for a couple of years. It would have made the owner's system more efficient and use less energy. But the owner refused to buy it. Two years later the owner admitted to the salesman that he had made a mistake, that he should have listened to the salesman earlier. Wow! That takes humility and a healthy ego.

When I became popular after I published my first book, *The Funnel Principle*, my ego made me think I was a superstar. I coveted flying business class overseas. I worked long hours, which was necessary, yet I wasn't present when I was home with my family. I was too busy—or thought I was too important—to get involved in my community and church life, but not too busy to build a big expensive house—a monument to my ego. I fought every day to protect a public image of success that I wanted everyone to see. I tried to be somebody that I really wasn't. I misled myself. Ego was there every step of the way.

As you age you should do less fighting because it's not necessary. I'm not saying that sales executives should stop ladder-climbing their careers, and I'm not suggesting we all retire at 50 and become yoga instructors. You can still climb and achieve and work hard, long hours when you have to and get there by taking a different route. Unfortunately, dialing back your fighting and passion is highly unlikely to happen because you've spent decades fighting. It's what is familiar to you and it's helped you succeed and get what you want. If you stopped cold turkey, you'd be turning your back on your ego. Why in the world would you do that?

Most people don't dial back their ego because they can't see the blindspots. You don't see the vice in the virtue, the ego betraying you in these later years. The ego is not needed to do for us what we needed it to do as we grew and developed and survived. You don't realize this, so ego hangs around looking for something to do. And it keeps doing what it does best—keeping you focused on you.

In this next phase, we have an opportunity to wake up and call out our ego for overextending itself because **all fighters get wounded**. There are no exceptions. Again, I'm not talking physical wounds, but rather emotional ones. And when we get emotionally wounded we usually don't handle that well, thanks to our ego. Men in particular. Maybe because, as Richard Rohr writes, it's common for men to have "daddy wounds," that is, emotional struggles related to things that fathers did or didn't do when the boys were growing up.

Everyone gets emotionally wounded, usually more than once, both men and women. Robert Downey, Jr., had much success as a young actor and singer, only to dive into drugs and alcohol before entering rehab and taking back his career. Patrick Kennedy, the former representative and son of Senator Ted Kennedy, in his book, *A Common Struggle*, describes drinking to endure the pains that he dealt with. Martha Stewart let greed get the best of her at one point.

This cycle of emotional wounding repeats for most people throughout life. You fight, you get wounded, you hurt, you ignore or deny it, you move on. You get wounded again, you hurt, etc. It happens often. Over time each event or episode builds on the other like a concrete callous. You don't let anything get through. You're a warrior doing what warriors do.

I saw a healthy ego in an emotionally distraught client a few years ago. I watched him, a CEO, go through a nasty divorce. He had wealth and the ex-wife's attorneys convinced her to take as much of it as she could. At one point he said to me, "I'm just over all of this." He really didn't care how much she took anymore. They beat him down. He demonstrated a healthy ego by not getting drawn into the emotional battle. The ex-wife's attorneys were all about the fight, about taking as much blood as they could. They worked from the unhealthy ego.

When we are wounded we often ignore or deny the messages that are trying to break through. Facing the problem can bring a lot of pain. Trying to deal with the pain over time brings suffering. The way we deal with the pain and suffering is 100% individual and unique, and yet patterns emerge. Some succumb to drinking. Some eat too much. Some become unfaithful. Some lose faith. Some get angry. Some act that out on others. Some retreat and hide. When I had my Singapore moment I wanted it to go away fast. I didn't want anyone to know about it. I wanted to deny it happened. I wanted to get back to being self-absorbed.

Blindspots: The Hidden Killer of Sales Coaching

Experiencing the Gift

While everyone gets wounded, not everyone allows themselves to be transformed by it or to learn from it. If you do embrace this transformation, you reach the next phase. **This is maturity.** Your ego has found a new role in a familiar home. It's like the feeling you experience if you've ever gone back to visit your childhood home or town. You never see it the same way. Everything looks smaller than you remembered. The distances to get places are shorter. You've taught your ego to forgive more, to be more humble, to think of others more than you think of yourself. My friend, author and keynote speaker Brian Biro, says humility is not that you think less of yourself; you just think of yourself less.

Richard Rohr makes it clear in his book, *Falling Upward,* that this suffering and falling from being wounded is not only necessary for transformation but it is the gift. It's an open door to get out of the hell you might be living in. But you need to walk through it. Like the vice in the virtue, it is a paradox. The answer lies somewhere inside. It's not black or white, left or right, light or dark, or whatever either/or image you want. It's both/and.

My son asked me recently if I wished I hadn't built that million dollar house and lived that lifestyle for several years. I immediately said, no I don't because I have a lot of good memories of that time and it gave me a ton of priceless lessons.

The last phase is wisdom. Here, the ego has comfortably been operating at a slower pace for some time. You're not threatened by the things that used to threaten you. There's little need to fight. The singer Steve Earle says in the song "Steve's Hammer" (for Pete Seeger), *"One of these days I'm gonna lay this hammer down, leave my burden resting on the ground."* On the surface, an outsider might think he sees the reason for someone entering the wisdom phase. The outsider thinks it has to do with receiving a nice pension, or paying off the house mortgage, or having grandkids. These milestones might influence wisdom but they in no way guarantee a deeply changed mind or heart that sees differently.

I really enjoy coaching younger managers. They rarely have the wisdom that a life of experiences provides. There's so much to share with them, but they have to learn it themselves. The columnist Peggy Noonan might describe their behavior as if "they've seen the movie but they haven't read the book." I tell them that when they encounter the challenging situation with a salesperson, instead of rushing to figure out how to fix it, take the time to learn what the moment is trying to teach them. There's something powerful that happens when you admit and confront your selfish behavior. You feel better. It's like pulling a drain plug out of a dirty sink and watching the swirling dirty water disappear.

The Ugly Trio: Selfishness, Control, and Fear

We have blindspots and we get in our own way because of what I call the ugly trio of selfishness, fear and control.

Selfishness

At the heart of getting in our own way is our selfishness. For most people it's human nature to be somewhat selfish. You have to be selfish to survive. It's when your selfishness grows out of balance that you get in your own way. Unfortunately this often happens without our being aware of it—it's a (yes, you guessed it) blindspot.

Often we see insecurity behind the motivations of selfishness. When someone isn't comfortable in their skin and with who they are, they can behave selfishly. I knew a salesperson whose selfishness and insecurity was so bad that she routinely blamed others for problems that she created. She would scream at everyone when she didn't get her way. Pretty soon, emails and accusations were flying like missiles throughout the entire headquarters. Someone with authority would be dragged in to defuse the situation. Then, a few months would go by and she'd initiate another episode. I honestly, and without judgment, think she had emotional and mental issues.

Passion is often a disguise for selfishness. I knew a sales director who had strong opinions for improving the business, but his colleagues and superior resisted his attempts to spark change. It's not that they disagreed with some of the changes, but they often struggled with his tactics. He was a rip-off-the-band-aid kind of guy when he should have been gently, slowly pulling back the edges. Some of his ideas were quite good, but they lost credibility in his "passionate" delivery. Most people he interacted with thought he was insincere and selfishly motivated.

Taking Responsibility

A mature ego takes responsibility for not only your actions but your reactions as well. Let's say you have a salesperson who gets under your skin routinely because he appears to make excuses. He still gets the work done and puts points on the board for your region, but he can be a handful. Some may call him high maintenance. Maybe the two of you don't emotionally connect. It's not a crime, but it is a block to greater performance. If you're conditioned to think, "Here comes another excuse" every time he opens his mouth, you're guaranteed to hear more excuses. It's a blindspot to immediately think you know what he's going to say and also to think you know the motivations behind it. In your head there's a voice that says, "He always responds like that," or "That's so typical of Bob."

When you take ownership of your response or reaction, you get better at coaching because you focus more on your response than on his behavior. I have a client who does this so well. She'll tell me about her interactions with others and I'm thinking, geez, that would drive me crazy and the first thing she says is, "I must be doing something wrong." That's owning the situation because she recognizes her part in the action-reaction equation. She needs to ask herself, Why does his behavior annoy me? Why does she think she responds the way she does when he behaves this way?

Here's a crazy idea—it's possible that her behavior actually inspires his behavior. Instead of a chicken and egg thing, it's an egg and chicken thing. If you look for the predictable pattern, you may find it more often than you think.

Control

Another thing that leads to getting in our own way is a desire to control things. Control can be important and valuable, like making sure an agenda for a sales meeting is precisely followed or the room set up is just so. Too often, however, our desire to control things is out of balance and unhealthy. It affects the people who are caught up in that and your coaching suffers.

I know a sales manager who was consumed by his need to control things. He carefully orchestrated meetings with his team to always go the way he planned. Topics that were "discussed" always ended with his points being right. "Debates" on issues were never really debates as much as they were platforms for reinforcing his policies and procedures. You might say he had no blindspot—he knew exactly what he was doing. He knew he was a control freak. He knew he manipulated people. The blindspot was in his thinking that somehow it was acceptable to treat people that way and that it would never come back to haunt him.

I know another manager who was very determined to implement certain policies that would affect people outside of her authority. She took every opportunity to make her case. She had such a strong personality that she even hijacked meetings that were not intended to discuss her views. She was blinded to what was so obvious to everyone else. What makes these blindspots even worse is the false positive of progress they create. Every yard of the field she advances against others gives her energy to continue the march. She alienated people in other departments. Some ended up leaving because they couldn't stand it any longer.

Insecurity can cause people to seize control. Those who allow controlling tendencies to dominate are afraid of what will happen if they don't control it. If you feel you have to be right, you fear not being right. If you have to win, you may not handle not winning very well. If you're too controlling of your salespeople, what do you think is the cause of your insecurity? What are you afraid that could happen?

There's a connection here to not knowing how to deal with being wounded, something I covered earlier in this chapter. Instead of dealing with wounds, people (take your pick) ignore them, deny them, hope they go away, or over compensate for them. And yet being wounded is a normal cycle of a person's life. We are all warriors in our own battles and it's inevitable that warriors will be wounded. If, however, we face the wounds head on and learn what the moment is trying to teach us, we'd likely reduce the amount of our own suffering.

Facing the wounds and the pain means giving up control. We're not sure where that will lead. It's no wonder we often choose to ignore when having a choice between ignoring and moving on or facing the pain and not knowing how long we'll suffer, or not knowing if we'll emerge more whole and repaired on the other side.

I tried to control lots of things for a long time. How my house was kept. What my kids did 24 hours a day. What time the dog was let out. What part of the lawn he pooped or peed on. Getting the family to church on time. Not to mention everything in my business. It steadily took a toll on me and everyone else. It's normal for controlling people to double down on the controlling behavior when things aren't going as they plan. That's as logical as AA members meeting at a bar. I was a mess.

Fear

If you're really honest with yourself, fear drives more of your life and what you do than you realize. I've witnessed many coaching calls where the behavior I saw was based on fear. Let me give you an example. I'm sure you've seen a salesperson make a sales call where she spends most of her time talking. She's not asking and learning. She's showing and telling. She likely does this to stay within a comfort zone, maybe one that's characterized by limited product or application knowledge. Part of me doesn't blame her. It's a survival tactic. But it will eventually cost her because she's not making any connection with the customer and won't easily make a sale. I've seen sales managers do the same thing.

A manager who is not comfortable leading her people to self-discovery or is fearful of asking questions doesn't coach effectively. A manager who is not comfortable with the possible answers that he doesn't have will not ask the questions and make himself vulnerable. As a result the sales person misses a learning opportunity. Worse, if that salesperson goes on to become a manager himself, he may model his own coaching on the fear-based, unquestioning way he was coached.

Another fear involves withholding information to keep the sales manager off the salesperson's back. Salespeople sometimes tell their sales managers only what the manager needs to hear. Clever, resourceful sales people have done that for years to survive managers who want to know everything. Today, with CRM, it's harder to play this game but it still happens. Sales managers play that same game with the people they report to, right? What do they fear? Another missed forecast? Getting called out on something that is embarrassing or a mistake?

Many times in my career as a consultant and coach I get to work with young managers and managers who are new to the position. Oftentimes these managers have veteran or older salespeople on the team and sometimes this dynamic leads to tension or worse. It's interesting to see the ego at play on both sides. Sometimes the veteran older salesperson feels more pressure in the situation and sometimes it is the manager who has more pressure. What does the veteran fear? That he'll be asked to change his ways? Does he fear having to learn something that takes him out of his routine or comfort zone of selling?

What could a young manager fear with one of his veteran, older sellers? Perhaps there's a fear of losing authority or credibility and other things within the hierarchical relationship that supposedly go with it. A young manager doesn't want salespeople colluding against him for whatever reason. There could also be a lot at stake for the young manager to perform well for his or her company. Maybe there's another promotion down the road.

Some fear comes from how we will see ourselves. Let me give you an example. I had a tense relationship with one of my children during her high school years. On the surface I was frustrated with her lack of tidiness and frequent procrastinating with school work. Nothing I said or did changed her behavior. My words usually made it worse. But I was determined to out-will her, and since I spent most of my time trying to "fix her," our relationship suffered.

After an exhausting length of time living this way, I had a breakthrough I never could have imagined. I realized that I was part of the problem! I didn't cause my daughter to procrastinate with school work or make her have a messy room. I contributed to our deteriorating relationship because I made it a mission to try to "fix" her. I told her as often as I could that we had expectations while living in our house and her behavior wasn't cutting it. So she avoided me. And when she couldn't, she compensated. One of the things I love about her is she's resourceful and a survivor.

My breakthrough was humiliating for me, which suddenly gave me a very unflattering view of myself. Like Churchill's character in *The Crown*, I thought, "I am that wretched and decaying man." Who wants to admit that? But I came to realize that I was often an intimidating, even angry, Dad. This verbally intimidating behavior of mine was not a show of love.

Start with Why

Here's a tough question for you: Are you a sales manager for the right reasons? This shouldn't come as a surprise, but if you're not suited to this role, you'll likely get in your own way often.

Becoming a sales manager may be something you aspired to for a long time. But when you think about the role of salesperson versus sales manager, in some ways they couldn't be more different. The accepted view that it's a logical progression from salesperson to sales manager is something I get, but sort of don't understand. Sometimes, when a company promotes its top salesperson to be sales manager, they lose their best rep and they get an average manager. Not a good day at the office. Unfortunately, smaller companies can't always offer ambitious salespeople any promotable opportunities other than the management position.

It's normal for people to find themselves in positions and even careers that aren't a good fit. A roommate of my brother's in college, Thad, started out in consulting after getting an MBA. He's now a priest. Many people who go to law school end up as something else.

Should you conclude that you're not cut out to be a sales manager, there's absolutely no shame in this. But it would be tragic if you didn't do something about it. I've coached sales managers who were miserable in the job. While some left their companies, others were able to find different, more satisfying, positions in the same company.

Are you a sales manager because someone told you you'd be good at it? Are you a sales manager because it's part of your career plan to get increasingly more responsibility and to earn more money? Are you a sales manager because it's the last job you'll have before you retire in three years? Wouldn't you want to be a sales manager for the right reasons? Wouldn't your salespeople want you to be their manager for the right reasons?

How Do You Know If Sales Management Is Right for You?

At a minimum as a sales manager, you should find it satisfying to lead or work with other people. You should feel energized, not exhausted, after discussions with team members. You should naturally enjoy watching others succeed. You might even be a bit on the unselfish side, or at least not crave the limelight like you'd expect a star salesperson to.

Typical responsibilities of a sales manager include the following:

- Training people
- Resolving conflicts
- Listening, sometimes endlessly, to reps' explanations and sometimes excuses
- Dealing with reps who don't take coaching
- Dealing with unmotivated reps
- Coaching salespeople
- Leading a sales process
- Being an advocate for your people, especially fighting for corporate resources

- Working well with other departments like operations and marketing
- Routinely giving recognition for things done well
- Providing constructive criticism

I coached a sales manager once who was struggling with just about all of these tasks. One day, after a series of Funnel Audits we did with his team, I could tell something was not right. At dinner he seemed exhausted. He told me that he didn't think he was cut out for the job. He felt it was too stressful. Eventually, he took a sales position within the company. He's smiling a lot more these days.

Is How You See Yourself Based on How Others See You?

You can get in your own way if you've bought into what others think of you, especially when that is not who you really are.

My father-in-law, God rest his soul, told my wife when she applied for college that she'd make a great engineer. She subsequently took nearly four years of engineering courses before she realized she didn't want to be an engineer. She switched to marketing. (I know she's really still an engineer because she's the one the kids and I run to when the internet's down in the house.)

Sometimes we form lasting impressions based on our own misguided impression. When I left college I was dead set on working for three years and then getting my MBA before applying it to marketing or product management and working my way up. To start, I took the GMAT entrance exam—twice. My scores weren't high enough to enter the top programs. I didn't want to settle for less, so I gave that pursuit a mental vacation. I continued in sales positions, including management and training. Still, I harbored thoughts of getting into marketing. When I was laid off in a downsizing, my last corporate position, I even tried a little marketing consulting before realizing the obvious—I should start a sales training practice. Duh! I honestly don't know why I had such a blindspot with my career. You'd think that with the last name Sellers I would have figured out my calling a lot faster!

The Gift of Humility Can Hurt

When you get these breakthroughs that let you see how you get in your own way, it's not always a high-five moment. The revelation is liberating and humbling. Humility can be like taking a body blow. You've stripped another layer to reveal more truth about yourself. Often facing that truth isn't pretty. But with each layer you remove one more barrier that has protected you from the deeper truth.

Frasier Crane didn't want to face the fact that he was obsessed with putting on appearances. He was swept away by his vanity. What if Frasier admits he's obsessed with himself—what does he do then? He won't be throwing a party, I'm guessing. There's too much at stake to topple the life he created.

For me, accepting that getting an MBA and a career in marketing wasn't my calling really stung me. It stripped off a layer of myself, but it got me closer to the real me which opened the right doors.

We don't always have to have clarity to do what's next, but as long as we have clarity to be honest with ourselves, we'll do okay. Like the overwhelmed and frustrated sales manager I coached, having the clarity that sales management wasn't his calling was paramount. Sharing that with me, his personal coach, was a big deal.

For me, I finally trusted the clarity, albeit after a lot of shadow boxing, that low GMAT scores meant that top graduate business schools wouldn't want me. I trusted the clarity that I would do well owning my own business. That clarity, which has served me well for 20 years, finally seemed right.

What If You're a Sales Manager for the Wrong Reasons?

As I said earlier, the revelation of getting closer to your true self is both liberating and frightening. What do you do if you decide you're not cut out for the sales management position you're in right now?

First, I wouldn't jump to that conclusion. One thing you could do is talk in confidence with someone you trust. You don't even have to get into details or reveal everything. Opening up to someone about being less than fulfilled or unhappy in the job usually is therapeutic at a minimum. You may get asked some good questions that make you think about your situation.

Maybe it's not the role you're struggling with but rather, you're conflicted by your company or uninspiring boss. You might just need to be a sales manager for a company with a culture that better fits your style and needs.

Long term, if you're not ideal for sales management, I hope you begin to discern where you do belong—in sales, a corporate environment, or running summer camps for youth. Trust in the tough questions you ask yourself even when they continue to cause pain. It will eventually lead you to where you belong.

Summary

The raw material to be the kind of sales manager who can make a difference in the lives of your salespeople is within you. A manager who embraces humility and practices forgiveness is aware of the danger of coveting things, knows the evils of judging people and trying to fix them, appreciates the contradictions of life, and checks his or her ego at the door. To see more of this manager, you have to get out of your own way.

This isn't a journey for the meek. But it is a journey with riches beyond imagination.

Now let's explore *how* you get out of your own way.

4

How to Get Out of Your Own Way

"The very things we wish to avoid, neglect and flee from turn out to be the 'prima materia' from which all real growth comes."
– Andrew Harvey

"First there is the fall, and then we recover from the fall. Both are the mercy of God."
– Lady Julian of Norwich

Ebenezer Scrooge is a good example of a man who didn't know how to get out of his own way—until he fell hard. On the surface Scrooge was a successful businessman providing jobs for others. Underneath, he was a broken soul. With the help of the Ghosts of Christmas Past, Present and Future, Scrooge came to face the truth of the man he had become. And after his sleepless night, he was faced with a decision.

Though he didn't see it this way, Scrooge's suffering was a gift— the gift of falling, of being wounded. Without the fall there is no rise and renewal to becoming a better version of yourself. Without the fall Scrooge goes on living his selfish, self-absorbed life. The fall is the wakeup call. Responding correctly to your fall is the key to getting out of your own way.

How We Usually Respond Is How Not to Respond

Understandably, most people resist being wounded and falling. No spoiler alert needed here. Wounds are not much fun. Our response is usually to ignore the wounds, deny the wounds, or suppress the wounds.

When you think about how much emotional wounding and falling we experience in a lifetime, we must be remarkably resilient to withstand such pain. Instead of acknowledging and addressing our wounds, we repeatedly compensate by getting angry or defending our behavior or find relief in substances such as alcohol, drugs, food, etc. We take out our frustrations on others. This buys us time. The relief is always temporary, a respite until we are wounded again, respond like before, and it repeats.

This cycle, however, gets broken when you respond differently to the fall, when you get out of your own way and allow yourself to be transformed.

Last night I saw a story about a white woman who moved into a predominantly black neighborhood and immediately flew her confederate flag. This caused a lot of ire. Over time, neighbors erected fences to block the view. The woman installed a taller flag pole. She was interviewed by a local television station at the height of her behavior, and she said that the resistance to her flag made her beliefs even stronger—until she had a heart attack. Then, suddenly, coming to terms with her mortality, she told the interviewer that she was ashamed of the divisive stand she'd been taking with her neighbors. She took down the flag and asked for forgiveness. Mercifully, her neighbors gave it to her.

Of course, even a heart attack isn't enough for some people to wake up and see they are getting in their own way. But when it is, grace enters and does its thing.

Blindspots: The Hidden Killer of Sales Coaching

The Temptation to Fix It Fast

We get many opportunities to learn from falling because we fall a lot throughout our lives. But because we're usually in such a hurry to escape, we don't learn what the fall is trying to teach us.

The prophet Jonah fell and eventually learned what that was meant to teach him. I share this well-known story from the Old Testament, not to preach but rather to make a point. God told Jonah to go to Nineveh to preach to the people. Nineveh was the capital city of Assyria, a place that had become putrid and disgusting with immorality. Jonah didn't want to go because he likely saw it as a hopeless cause. He couldn't imagine why God would send him there to preach to people so lost and aimless. He thought he knew better than God what was best for him so instead of going to Nineveh, he boarded a ship to Tarshish. God wasn't happy with this decision.

Soon, the seas became dangerously stormy, putting the ship in peril. The ship's crew, when it discovered Jonah's situation, berate him and throw him overboard. Jonah is "saved" by a whale that swallows him whole. He does what anyone would do in this situation; he fights to get out. God tells Jonah not to fight his time in the belly of the whale but rather, to have faith that God will spit Jonah out onto a new shore when He is ready. Jonah surrenders and lives in the belly of the whale for three days and comes to terms with his poor decision to disobey God. Eventually Jonah is a transformed man.

Or maybe you prefer a pop culture story with a similar moral. There's a line in the song "Crystal Ball" by the artist Pink that goes like this:

I'm learning to be brave in my beautiful mistakes.
Oh I've felt that fire and I, I've been burned
But I wouldn't trade the pain for what I've learned
I wouldn't trade the pain for what I've learned.

I don't know Pink's motive for writing this song but I suspect she has experienced some falling in her life. Nonetheless, she wouldn't trade the pain of what those challenges taught her. Another word for this is wisdom.

Have you ever felt like you were in the belly of the whale? Maybe you didn't take enough time to understand why you were there. When you got out maybe you dusted yourself off, pulled yourself together, and went on living like nothing had happened.

Or maybe like Pink or Jonah you had a different response. You learned from it. You were changed. There was no going back. These are the gifts that are waiting for you if you get out of your own way.

Knowing why you get in our own way often requires you to do the exact opposite of what you really want to do. In the moment of being in the whale's belly, like Jonah, you want to run as fast and as far away from your troubles as possible. Deny or forget that whatever happened, happened. When I was in Singapore I wasn't interested in understanding my mess—I wanted to bury it and make it go away. I'm sure glad something got a hold of me and gave me the courage to surrender.

Since getting in your own way when coaching your salespeople appears as selfishness, fear and self-importance with a title, control, or a need to be right, or a need to not appear weak, the temptation might be to work on these behaviors. Maybe hire a personal coach. Take a class. Get some training. Learn some tips and techniques.

Any of those could be worthwhile. But these blindspot behavior flaws are just the exhaust fumes of the ego locomotive that steams down the tracks. Taming or even eliminating these behaviors comes from responding differently to your ego which is the root cause.

What makes this even more difficult is the vice in the virtue. I read where the billionaire, Dallas Mavericks' owner, and Shark Tank star Mark Cuban was mentoring the former Uber CEO Travis Kalanick during

Blindspots: The Hidden Killer of Sales Coaching

Kalanick's term as CEO. Cuban said the thing that's so impressive about Travis is he'd run through walls for you. And he said that the biggest problem for Travis is he'd run through walls for you. The virtue eventually becomes the vice.

To stop these unflattering behaviors that prevent better coaching and leadership you need to be vulnerable.

Vulnerability

What is vulnerability and what does it mean to be vulnerable?

Vulnerability is the capability of being physically or emotionally wounded.

I'm guessing that you aren't interested in signing up for that!

Brené Brown is a celebrated author of five #1 New York Times best sellers and leading expert on the topic of vulnerability. In her *Ted Talk,* which has some 39 million views, she says that vulnerability is shame, fear and the struggle to belong, connect and find worthiness in ourselves. But it's also the pathway to joy, creativity, belonging and love. When we numb our vulnerability to painful emotions, we also block our pleasurable emotions, such as joy, gratitude and happiness. Without vulnerability, we're miserable people, looking for purpose and meaning in life.

This is what being less vulnerable looks like for me. When I go to a party I plan an escape route. Usually that means I drive myself so I'm not dependent on someone else to take me home. I want that control. If I want to leave early, I do. I avoid the messiness associated with negotiating with the people who drove me or disappointing them by wanting to leave early or stay late.

While I prefer this controlled scenario, I realize that it's a burden. If I relaxed my need to control when I leave I would be more vulnerable, but I might actually have a better time and be more in the moment when

I'm there. My controlling behaviors, protect me from being vulnerable.

One of my clients, Kris Hardin, the Vice President of Commercial Services at Hunton Services in Houston, has been a model of embracing vulnerability. Over the five years I've coached Kris and his sales teams, he's been steadily more transparent in front of his people. As a result his people know him better. He has connected more deeply with them. He's allowed them to see a side of him that reveals the fuller picture of who he is. They respect his coaching and leadership because they understand more deeply where it comes from. He's earned the right to come down hard when he has to because they know he'll balance that with support and encouragement.

Kris wasn't always that vulnerable. Like many managers he used to cling to a notion that he always had to show the tough side of his personality. He had to always show that he was in control. Had to always show that he had the right answer and knew what to do. He and I talked about how being more vulnerable could create emotional connections that could motivate and inspire his team to greater performance. This was not easy for him to embrace. It helped when Kris realized that by being more vulnlerable he was simply letting out a part of him that had previously been denied. The paradox was, as it always is, that it required Kris to be more of himself.

Consequently, his results are amazing. His teams have delivered record-breaking revenue and operating income results for five years in a row.

On a personal note, it's fun to see Kris be more vulnerable because it's a beautiful contradiction seeing this physically imposing man, a 6'5" former college standout basketball player, display the strength of his humility and vulnerability.

Not being more vulnerable robs leaders of opportunities to make emotional connections with their people. Consider this example. A sales manager is preparing for a mid-year sales meeting with his region. The region is well over plan and he can connect the dots of their efforts to the results. He's feeling good, and his immediate thought is to spend time praising the team and recognizing people. This comes natural to him. But there's a hitch—his manager, the Vice President of Sales, will attend the meeting. And the VP is not the type who buys into a style of recognizing and praising. He prefers sticks to carrots all the time. The sales manager second guesses his instincts and worries that if he recognizes and praises, his boss will jump in and start hammering people for not doing enough. Then at the break or end of the day, the boss will pull him aside and coach him on why his approach was wrong.

The boss's presence convinces the sales manager to abandon his heart-felt initial plan and he drafts another agenda that focuses on pushing the team harder.

Resisting Vulnerability

Being vulnerable is something most people resist. For men in particular, from the time we are old enough to walk and talk we aren't taught to be vulnerable. We're taught the opposite. Being vulnerable implies that we are weak, a character flaw. Got a bully problem? Go punch the guy in the nose. Does your leg hurt from that rough tackle? Get up and get in the next play.

Being vulnerable can suggest that people will take advantage of us. We'll get screwed in a deal. Many traditional, popular negotiation tactics tell us to keep our cards close to our chest. I get that. But I also know many stories where being more transparent in the negotiation encouraged the other party to also be more transparent. As a result, trust builds trust. You might get to a better deal faster.

When I sold my house four years ago my selling agent also represented the buyer. Whoa, Mark, you're thinking, that can't be good. How does she serve my interest and his? Honestly, I didn't plan it that way and I had no idea how it would work. But we had an offer five days after listing. My agent called me with the buyer's low ball offer and I countered. She then said calmly and not in a pressuring way, "The buyer doesn't want to play games. He wants to know what's it going to take to buy your house?" I embraced my vulnerability and asked for her opinion since she seemed like she had my back. With her input we settled on a number. I thought it was fair but also aggressive. I wasn't sure he'd pay this premium but I trusted her advice. The agent took my counter to the buyer, then came back and said, "We have a deal."

I have good feelings about my experience with my agent. I also have a good relationship with the buyer, which isn't common. He and I run into each other occasionally in town. He personally brings me my un-forwarded mail. We talk like friendly acquaintances.

Vulnerability Doesn't Define Us

As the father of two daughters I'm sensitive to my girls being vulnerable. I want them to be strong, independent women with positive outlooks on life. I don't want people to take advantage of them. I don't want vulnerability to backfire. As the father to a son I know my boy is surrounded by anti-vulnerable peer pressure images. Boys aren't taught to show emotions, like crying or hugging. We're conditioned to suppress these things. Have you seen Jimmy Valvano's 1993 speech at the ESPY awards? There wasn't a dry man's eye in the place.

Both men and women avoid being vulnerable to protect the beliefs and positions that they use to define themselves. When something doesn't fit our belief or position, the ego tells us to fear and defend. The ego wants us to think in terms of either-or, black or white, left of right, you're either with me or you're against me. It's the dualistic mindset. We like categories because they help us know how to deal with others.

Blindspots: The Hidden Killer of Sales Coaching

Quickly. We think this insularity keeps us safe. What it does is imprison us. It's small minded. It leaves no space for seeing others for the unique people they are. Consequently we don't grow, we don't positively impact others. We don't contribute as much to the world around us as we could.

Brené Brown tells a story about someone at one of her conferences trying to define her based on her Texas roots. Upon learning that she is from Texas the person immediately said some things that suggested everyone knows what people from Texas are like—gun toting, cocky, conservatives who have no empathy or liberal-leaning bones in their bodies. Man, did she take offense and put this person in his place. "You have no idea who I am," she scolded him.

If you think you have your salespeople well-defined, you'll risk taking them for granted and not seeing them for the unique people they are. It will prevent you from making an emotional connection. Here's one way to avoid this mistake. At your next region meeting play an icebreaker called 'truth and lies'. Each person writes on a piece of paper two things that are true about themselves and one thing that is not true. Then take turns in pairs trying to figure out which of the three is the lie. I did this once and learned that one guy really did speak Mandarin Chinese and another guy could actually dead lift 350 pounds!

Context, however, is important when being vulnerable. I'm not advocating that you reveal all aspects or secrets of your life story to your sales team. They're not your therapy group. But the relationship with your salespeople is a personal one, whether you want it to be or not. When you let them get to know you better, they'll let you get to know them better.

Get to Know Your Players Bert

Knowing your salespeople better will help you create better emotional connections and get more of what you want from them. In a scene from the movie, *The Blindside*, about the American football player Michael Oher, Michael is not doing what the coach, Bert, is yelling at him to do. Leanne, Michael's adopted mother character played by Sandra Bullock, interrupts the football coach's practice to talk to Michael. Bert is flabbergasted but steps aside. Leanne reminds Michael that the quarterback and running back are family and his job is to protect them just as he protects his adopted family. (In an earlier scene where Michael crashes the car he is driving, with his adopted younger brother in the front seat, he reaches over at the point of impact to stop the airbag from exploding into the young brother).

On the next several plays Michael blocks like a beast and mows over the defensive tackles. The coach is stunned. He walks to the stands where Bullock is sitting and sheepishly asks, "Okay, what'd you say to him?" Bullock replies, "You should get to know your players, Bert. Yelling at him doesn't work. He doesn't trust men. He tested 98% on protective instincts." While Bert's 'be a man' coaching fell flat with Michael, I give him credit for being vulnerable enough to step aside and let Leanne save the day.

Asking others to be more vulnerable in your desire to know them better often happens when you go first. I attended a private workshop conducted by Mike Bosworth, creator of the classic sales book, *Solution Selling*, a while back. The workshop was for his new book and system called What Great Salespeople Do, and to my surprise, Bosworth showed us that great salespeople are vulnerable. He said when we go first in showing vulnerability others are more likely to respond similarly. This creates an emotional connection. In all my years of sales training this was one of the biggest paradoxes I had ever heard. I now practice this all the time.

On a recent business trip that started with a 6 am flight, I checked into the hotel after a long day with a client, including dinner. I was tired.

Blindspots: The Hidden Killer of Sales Coaching

When the hotel employee asked me how I was doing I was honest, not complaining, and said I was very tired. She went on to say she could relate. She'd been up all night with her infant son the previous night. We smiled and briefly enjoyed the human connection that probably, and ironically, gave each of us a slight energy boost.

When you are vulnerable you give others an invitation to share in your emotions. In one of my coaching calls with a sales manager, he told me about the Honor Flight he recently took with his father. The Honor Flight is an organization that takes war veterans to Washington, DC for a day to tour war memorials and to hang out with other veterans. Toward the end of the manager's story he paused and told me that he was getting emotional recounting the trip. I was moved that he shared that with me. It made me think fondly of my father in law, a WWII veteran, who took an Honor Flight several years earlier. The manager and I had one more meaningful connection binding us.

Being Vulnerable Leads to Greater Sales Performance

Because vulnerability will make you a better version of you, you will soon be a better version of the sales manager you're meant to be. You'll develop deeper connections with your people. The more deeply you connect with them, the more you will get out of them. You'll gain more credibility and you'll win over skeptics, including those who wanted your job when you interviewed for it. You'll become a better, more authentic listener, and your salespeople will recognize and appreciate this. When you need to use the stick instead of the carrot, your salespeople will respond appropriately. They won't misinterpret your harsh criticism or tough love as something it's not, such as judgment or selfishness. They'll see it for what it is—care and concern for them. They'll sell more for you. Just ask Kris Hardin of Hunton Services.

I hope you're wondering how to put this into practice. Let's see how you can get out of your own way.

Be Aware of How You Come Across to Your Salespeople

If you're like most people, the first time you hear your voice played back on audio or video, you are surprised at how it sounds. Isn't it odd that something we hear all the time, every time we speak, doesn't sound the way we hear it?

In a similar way you might be surprised at how you come across to your salespeople. How they experience you can have a lasting impact on them. Since we tend to have a more flattering image of ourselves than what is true, you could be coming across to your people in ways that surprise you and that is hurting your coaching.

I like telling this funny story about my father Monty and how he came across to a friend of mine, Ned. Monty, the friend and I were playing golf years ago. On the 3rd and 4th holes I made birdies. My friend was giving me high fives. When I made birdie on the 5th hole, my third birdie in a row he was really excited. I admit I was a little amped up too. I was a competitive golfer in college but still it's not common to do that. While Ned was giving me high fives Dad was stone cold stoic. Not an ounce of emotion. I then birdied the next two holes to make it five in a row and by now Ned was roaring with praise. Still Dad didn't say a word.

When Ned told this story in the company of friends and some beers several weeks later, he said, "And you should have seen Monty. Boy was he pissed!" I was shocked by my friend saying this. Nothing could have been further from the truth. Dad was my biggest fan during my competitive golf days. While being pissed was not accurate, still that's how Dad came across to Ned. Dad's stoic expression was his way of not wanting me to get too excited and not let the moment go to my head. As a somewhat serious guy myself, I can relate, but I understand why Ned would not.

Blindspots: The Hidden Killer of Sales Coaching

I validated my Dad's blindspot by sharing this story with him. When I asked him if he was pissed he thought that was absurd. When I asked Dad why he thought that Ned would think that he had no idea. Welcome to a blindspot Dad!

When coaching your salespeople over the phone, sometimes the phone isn't flattering to your traits. I had a sales manager client once whom I could barely hear when he was leading Funnel Audits. His energy level seemed very low. It was tempting to get the impression that he didn't want to be there and didn't care much about the Audit and the salesperson. Later I asked him if he was feeling okay and told him what I observed.

Another manager client of mine, many years ago, had a habit of pausing a long time before he would comment after his salespeople made a comment. This might not be an issue when face to face, but over the phone when the only element that binds the conversation is verbal, I found it disruptive. It was especially obvious when the salesperson said something that I thought deserved a quick "atta boy" or a confirming kind of reply. One of the reps said, "I was finally able to get in to see so and so after six months of trying," and the manager paused, probably reflected and then said, "Why isn't this opportunity on your funnel?" The manager just peed on his parade. The manager would have made an emotional connection had he immediately replied, "Hey, that's great! I can't believe he finally agreed to meet you," or "Wow, there's a lesson in persistence! Way to go." I asked the manager after the call if he noticed this flow of dialogue, and especially did he notice the rep getting quiet after that exchange. He hadn't.

It's surely frustrating when you are just being you and your behavior has a negative impact on others. Add to that your blindspot about this and the repeated offenses and you can see how blindspots can be complex. Of course you should be yourself to be authentic. But if your authenticity comes off as arrogance, standoffishness, insincerity, selfishness, emotional detachment, disinterest, judgment, jealousy, or interrogation, then your authenticity will be as welcomed as a hot bowl of soup in Phoenix in August. Your coaching and leadership will suffer. The paradox of this either makes it clear for you, or further befuddles you. As Jordan Peterson says, "The you that you think is you isn't you. It's your ego." This means that what people sometimes see from you is not your authentic self, but rather someone you are trying to be, either consciously or subconsciously. It also means that your authentic self is sometimes being hijacked or held hostage and just can't get out. But it's still in you! Your authenticity is a die cast yet the ego is so powerful as to not let us see it in its entirety.

To be clear, letting the rest of you come out will often take a ton of work, lots of shadow boxing to understand the contradictions, and lots of pain and suffering. If you're committed to the work, you can do it.

Acknowledge That You Contribute to the Problem

To get out of your own way it's important to acknowledge that your behavior, in some way, contributes to the behavior of your salespeople. This can be very hard to understand and accept.

Let's go back to the relationship with my daughter during her high school years. Because she didn't always do what I asked her to do around the house, I chose to spend all my time trying to fix her. Being the tough and smart survivor she is, she avoided me. I devoted the little time we spent together to trying to fix her and, therefore, this dominated our relationship. I easily justified my behavior by telling myself it was how I was raised. Now I was the parent. I provided many things to give her a fulfilling life. This is how the contract works.

Looking back, I think being more vulnerable would have looked like me dropping the attitude of "it's my house, I set the rules, you obey them." I could have just had a logical conversation with her about the need to chip in for the family and everyone pulls his own weight. I could have done a lot more to communicate the obvious—that I cared deeply about her and I had no idea what it was like to be in high school today let alone what it's like to be a young woman in high school. I should have been doing more listening and learning and showing love to balance the toughness I was showing. As proof that even the most sensitive of relationships can be mended, my daughter and I now have a terrific relationship because of the steps I took to recognize, apologize and be much less judgmental.

One of my clients realized that he was contributing to one of his salespeople struggles to embrace the new sales process we had trained him and his colleagues in. In our monthly Audit calls the salesperson seemed lost. He lacked confidence and he couldn't connect the dots, which frustrated the manager. We tried to get to a root cause. Did the salesperson need to understand expectations better? Did he need more training? Did he lack motivation?

I asked the manager a tough question: *How do you think Stephen would describe the Audit with you?* Then I asked, *Is it possible he's uncomfortable in this setting?*

To the manager's credit, instead of reacting defensively to my question he was open to the possibility that he was contributing to his rep's behavior.

The manager said that when he meets with Stephen in his office, for just about any reason, they have good conversations and he is relaxed. I guessed that the manager is relaxed, too. Nothing's getting in the way of a good conversation.

We decided to do the next month's Funnel Audit call with Stephen in the manager's office. I attended by phone. The first thing the manager did was apologize to Stephen for making the past calls difficult. He took ownership. He was vulnerable. Then he focused on just having a conversation, within the format and structure of our process.

The conversation was fantastic. I was so proud of the manager for his openness to change and the courage to be more vulnerable. Stephen, by way, has climbed to number one in the company.

Unfortunately, blindspots can be overwhelming for some people to overcome. I once knew a sales manager for a medical device company who struggled mightily to be empathetic and caring. He didn't seem to have that bone in his body. He came across as cold and too much all business all the time. He seldom smiled. He looked distrusting. When I listened to his coaching conversations with his reps, there was always this tension and heaviness in the air. His reps couldn't connect with him. Not a lot of coaching took place on these calls. Instead, he did a lot of process preaching and know-it-all managing. Regretfully, I couldn't get through to him in my coaching despite much effort, and eventually he was fired.

Tame Your Judgment

You get in your own way when you judge your salespeople. Unfortunately, judging people is a common, unflattering behavior that we all are guilty of.

You know what judgment looks like. Have you ever sat in church and heard a baby wailing and thought, *how can the mom or dad of that baby be so inconsiderate? Why don't they go to the cry room?* Why don't we think instead, *It's so impressive that this young mother has the energy and commitment to get her kids to church on Sunday.*

Or, have you ever waited a long time at a fast food restaurant and when it's time for the person in front of you to order, she doesn't know what she wants? Have you ever thought, *You've been in line for ten minutes and you don't know what to order?* What the mind is really

Blindspots: The Hidden Killer of Sales Coaching

thinking is, *How stupid can you be?*

One of the blindspots some managers have is passing judgment on a salesperson who doesn't do sales like the manager used to do sales. Let's say you're super organized and you have a salesperson who is not. It would be reasonable for you to lose your patience after repeated coaching to help him be more organized. But it would be judging him if you thought that he's not as serious about his job as an organized person, like you.

One of the best things you could do is to stop to consider the possibility that a rep can be successful despite having poor organization skills. This would tame your judgment. Then, you could ask your rep how important he thinks it is to be organized. You'll know you're being genuine if you don't have a reply already crafted. Just listen. Ask him to describe what being organized looks like. Ask him how organized he thinks he is. Most importantly, ask him if he would want you to help him be organized. This is important. I tell managers that they have the right to manage their salespeople—they're the boss—but they don't have the right to coach their salespeople. That has to be earned.

When you think you have someone all figured out, this is a blindspot. When this person is someone whose behavior you don't click with, your judgment is likely to get through. For example, maybe you think you can anticipate everything she's about to say ("that's so like her to say something like that") and everything she's about to do ("I'm never surprised by her.") It gets worse when you think you know her motives, which sort of throws fuel on the fire of your bias. You may tell yourself you're a great judge of character. You're impressed with your "knack for reading people." This is a dangerous blindspot because there's a chance you've permanently written this person off. You give her no chance at redemption. It's a death sentence. Your coaching calls are likely anything but productive. She may be just as uncomfortable with you as you are with her.

Judging the Basher

As you might expect, I've had many sales manager clients struggle to put up with salespeople who complained a lot about the company's problems. They're usually accurate that the company has problems, and I try to gently remind everyone that every company has problems. I recall one manager that had a salesperson who would hijack every conversation as an opportunity to complain. This fatigued the manager. That stress and fatigue can lead to a lot of passing judgment like thinking the rep cared for no one but himself (sometimes true, sometimes not true), or he hates our company (not accurate), or is acting like a big jerk (ok, maybe a little true).

Ironically, some of these managers made the situations worse by trying to shut down the salesperson and discount their opinions and feelings before the salesperson was fully heard. They should have been more empathetic and acknowledging of the rep's criticism. But I also believe in a shelf life for being heard. You can't let a salesperson repeatedly bring up issues that have already been expressed and that have plans in place to be dealt with. Managers need to step in to get the conversation back to its original purpose. I've also seen managers that do not contain a vocal salesperson's relentless criticism and it spreads like a Lake Erie toxic bloom in Toledo. Everyone on the team is expecting the manager to deal with it and when he doesn't his credibility takes a hit.

Stop Trying to Fix Your Salespeople

I shared with you my attempt to fix one of my children during high school because I judged her and behaviors I didn't like. What a lesson that was. One of my wife's favorite *TED Talks*, by Ken Robinson, is called,

Blindspots: The Hidden Killer of Sales Coaching

"Are Schools Killing Creativity?" At one point it was the most viewed *TED Talk* of all time. Late in the talk Robinson gets to the story of Gillian Lynne, an eight-year-old girl who couldn't concentrate in her school setting. The school's administrator wrote to Lynne's parents and said Gillian has a learning disorder. And because she can't sit still, her restlessness is bothering others. They recommended that the parents take her to see a specialist.

At the doctor's office the mother and doctor talked for 20 minutes about the things the school said Gillian was doing wrong. The doctor then told Gillian he needed to speak privately to the mother in another room. Before he left the room he turned on a radio that was playing music and left the door open.

When they left the room the doctor instructed the mother where to stand so she could watch her daughter. Gillian was on her feet, moving to the beat of the music. The doctor turned to the mother and said, "Mrs. Lynne. Gillian isn't sick. She's a dancer. Take her to a dance school."

It's a good thing Gillian's mother didn't see Gillian as a problem to be fixed, like the school did, because Gillian Lynne did become a dancer. She graduated from the Royal Ballet in London. She then became a choreographer and choreographed some of the most successful broadway shows in history, seen by millions of people around the world including, *The Phantom of the Opera* and *Cats*.

Unfortunately, I've seen many sales managers who think their salespeople are problems to be fixed.

Viewing someone as a problem to be fixed sets up a negative relationship between a manager and a salesperson. There's a good chance the relationship is doomed before it even begins. It's not hard to imagine the manager treating the salesperson in an unflattering, even disrespectful manner. Remember, like a dog that smells fear, salespeople have good senses too. They know when their manager thinks of them in such a negative way.

Funny thing, too, when you think about it—who endowed a manager with the gift to identify and fix a salesperson? That's the ego in control.

One manager client of mine made it her mission to fix a lot of people on her team. Instead she made a lot of enemies. Her region suffered high turnover. Some that stayed were unhappy and unmotivated. Despite her region making its numbers during the years I worked with her, eventually she was asked to leave. Her strong personality and unrelenting mindset alienated too many people.

Just being the sales manager doesn't give you the authority to coach your people. When you have an underperforming salesperson you might be tempted to apply lots of pressure coaching. But you might be wasting your time. It might surprise you to hear that I've met many salespeople that are content with their average or under performance and not eager to improve. This complacency doesn't sit well with me or the manager I'm working with. Sometimes the underperforming, unmotivated seller is married to someone who makes the bank in the house and the underperformer would rather be doing something else. I'm tempted to jump to a conclusion that these people must be lazy. I'll be honest when I say that I struggle to draw the line at times between lazy behavior and just plan lazy.

I coached a salesperson several years ago who was a minority share owner of his company. He would not follow the sales process we trained the entire company in. After considerable effort I was still clueless regarding his behavior. Eventually, he told me what was going on. Simply, he was content with his level of performance and his style and income. It didn't matter to him that his performance was not meeting requirements by the majority share owner. This helped me understand much better how to approach this person.

Don't think I'm saying you have to live with the team you have or have inherited and ride them till they retire or leave or expire. To be clear, if you have salespeople who are not performing for reasons of attitude or ability, you have a decision to make. Either you invest in making them better or they become a necessary ending and you let them go. It's your team and it's your responsibility to hit your number.

Diving For Pearls

Another way to get out of your own way is to stop assuming you know what motivates your sales people and instead find the pearls they are diving for.

In the late 1800s pearls were treasured jewels. They had to be gathered by divers descending hundreds of feet to the floors of oceans. In some countries usually these divers were women. It was an extremely risky profession. They routinely risked hazards such as ocean creatures, waves, and blacking out due to lack of oxygen. The technology was crude. Divers might use a heavy rock to preserve energy on the descent. They might coat their bodies with animal fat to prevent hypothermia. Why did these men and women risk so much? Maybe for some it was a job that provided for family. Maybe it was something they learned from someone in the family. Maybe some were carrying on a tradition. Maybe some felt obligated and proud. Maybe some were trying to get bragging rights. And maybe some just loved finding pearls.

What are the pearls your salespeople are diving for? It's tempting to assume that since they're in sales, the pearls are earning money. When you explore beyond that, you often find that the motivations are rooted in personal things that drive the behavior. If a salesperson wants to make a lot of money because he wants to prove to his family that he can be successful, then it's really not about the money, is it? If a salesperson wants to be a sales manager and knows that she has to prove success as a rep first, then the motivations are more about the promotion and what that means to her.

Be curious about these motivations. More than likely, given all the time you spend with your salespeople, they will give you signs of their pearls all the time.

The Need for Self-Awareness

Being a sales manager is a high-stress job. It probably feels like you're juggling 15 spinning plates, half of them wobbling precariously and close to crashing to the ground. At a minimum, a typical week includes somebody on your team frustrating you, or letting you down, or a crisis with marketing or operations or the technical staff. You're not just in the center—you're the hub. All of this activity flows through you. And when a rep repeatedly commits the same mistakes, or does something most people would feel is not exercising good common sense, you're tempted to react in ways that don't create an emotional connection. As a result, you're less likely to get what you want.

Embracing your vulnerabilities will bring you more self-awareness and allow you to get out of your own way faster and more gracefully. Steadily you'll be winning the way with your blindspots.

5

Staying Out of Your Own Way

"This invisible power, the power of the other, builds both the hardware and the software that leads to healthy functioning and better performance."
–Dr. Henry Cloud, leadership expert, psychologist, and best-selling author

"No wise person ever wanted to be younger."
– Native American aphorism

By now, you've learned why you get in your own way and you know how to get out of your own way. So how do you stay out of your own way?

The bad news is you cannot stay out of your own way once and for all and forever. A healthier mindset is to replace that destination or goal with setting your sights on "being your best today." That's doable for everyone and a lot less overwhelming. Over time, all of these daily victories add up to a lifelong narrative of creating emotional connections and getting what you want and need.

Make Sure You Are Where You Belong

It's a big challenge to stay out of your own way if you struggle with the job of leading salespeople. In her book Grit, Angela Duckworth tells us that 50% of West Point graduates leave the military immediately after their five year commitment is over. Apparently, the military is not a good fit for those that leave. If you're a manager and you're struggling to enjoy the challenge, don't be disheartened. It takes a special type of person, not necessarily a better one, to want to lead and manage salespeople. There's no shame in finding out that you're not one of these people.

As a manager, your first responsibility is to your people, not to yourself. You cannot succeed without them succeeding. This is a striking difference between selling and managing and yet we see top sellers promoted to managers all the time.

The sales manager must focus his energies on lifting others. He needs to know the pearls his people are diving for and understand what gets them down emotionally. He has to want to get personal. He must want to care. A president once told me, in sharing his frustration and assessment of one of his sales managers, "I just don't think Ron cares about his people." A tough thing to say, but possibly true. If Ron did care, it didn't appear that way to his president. A blindspot.

The sales manager must be part psychologist, part coach, part parent, part buddy, and part hard ass, and also know when to play these roles. He must get in each salesperson's head and motivate and influence each one. Columbus Blue Jackets hockey head coach John Tortorella was very good at this in the 2017 season. At mid-year he "healthy scratched" the team's top goal scorer of the previous season, Cam Atkinson. The week before, Atkinson had signed a $40M contract. But he wasn't performing this week, so Tortorella benched him. When a reporter asked the coach what he said to Atkinson, the coach replied, "I didn't need to say anything to him. He knows what to do." In other words, getting benched sent the message, but so did the coach's lack of words.

Blindspots: The Hidden Killer of Sales Coaching

Put in the Time

Not only do you have to want to stay out of your own way, you have to work at it. Love your wife? Better work at showing her. Love your parents? Don't let it be an unspoken understanding. Do something to show that love.

I'd like to get my golf handicap back to low-single digits. I don't have that motivation in me right now to put in the time. I'd rather do a dozen other things. I'm at peace with that.

One manager I coached came up with a clever way to stay out of his own way. He had a tendency to talk over his salespeople during sales calls so he gave himself a budget of asking no more than three questions when he would ride with them. I love the intention.

To change your blindspot behavior, you need to get to the root cause. Like a sore spot on your body if it's sensitive or uncomfortable to deal with, you're probably on the right track to knowing the source. I decided several years ago that I was not happy being average with my faith life. When I was brutally honest with myself I became ashamed that I wouldn't tolerate mediocrity in my profession and hobbies but for my faith, apparently, I was okay drawing the line there. Not my proudest moment. It humbled me. But I'm also proud of facing this and acting on it. I steadily made several commitments over the next few years to turn this around, and it's paid off. I'm more at peace, more fulfilled, a much better role model to those who know me, and I'm spiritually healthier than ever.

In the end, you have to really want it. You'll have to sacrifice to get it.

Humility as a Way of Life

There's nothing I can say from experience that has more impact on staying out of your own way than practicing humility. Candidly, I don't think of humility when I think of salespeople. Our profession is not one where humility comes easy. The humble sellers I've met are like diamonds in the rough. Sales seems to reward only selfish behavior, but this is a myth.

Though you've probably been graced by some humble people you might be tempted to think it's a character trait that you either have or don't have. I suggest you see it more as a way of life. It's within reach of everyone to do things daily that express humility. You can be of service to people who aren't as fortunate as you. You can get involved in your local food bank, for example, or any of the many outreach activities your local place of worship provides. Volunteer your talents. Your humility provides the counterweight to your self-centeredness. Many of you already do this. You're heroes.

There's a saying that I've heard used when someone reflects on their life or legacy that goes, how you live your life is how you live your days. Every day everyone has the same opportunity to be more humble. Don't let it happen by accident. When I hear really good coaching there's often a healthy dose of humility behind it.

Build a Team

Staying out of your own way is more likely to happen when you admit that you can't do life alone.

You aren't created to go through life alone. Many studies show that married people live longer and healthier lives. Prisoners in solitary confinement are shown to emerge with serious and sometimes irreversible mental effects from the isolation. Enneagram types that struggle to connect emotionally with others, like 5s who won't let others get too close, and 8s who resist being vulnerable, create problems for themselves. Again we have a vice in the virtue dynamic that can lead to a blindspot.

Consider surrounding yourself with a personal team that helps you become a better version of yourself. This team could be comprised of people that feed your spiritual needs, that keep you humble, that love you unconditionally, look after you, hold you accountable, and otherwise keep your compass needle pointed at true north.

This can be hard for people in sales because they are often independent and isolated types. They're making sales calls mostly by themselves. Many salespeople might not even have an office outside of their home office. That physical isolation is now paired with an emotional isolation. The solo drive and ambition that is often necessary to thrive in sales builds a wall around them. If all of this isolation and independence seems natural - it's certainly a virtue - then guess what? Sooner or later it will be a vice.

One way to build a team is to hire a personal coach. Someone that might help you with setting goals for your life and career, for both your physical and spiritual health. I have the privilege of being a coach who helps clients become better sales leaders and better men and women. The boundary between work and personal life is often blurred or even nonexistent so my clients end up working on both.

One of my favorite books about building your personal team is, *The Power of the Other*, by Henry Cloud. In this book Dr. Cloud explores the relationships that shape our lives, for better or worse. He writes that it's "The Corner 4 relationships" that you want to create, and defines them as Corner 1: no connection, Corner 2: bad connection, Corner 3: pseudo connection and Corner 4: real connection. Your Corner 4 people are the people that help you become a better version of yourself.

One source of Corner 4 relationships is through faith grouping. These are small groups of men or women that meet regularly to deepen their spirituality and religious beliefs. These groups are a wonderful means of engaging in sisterhood or brotherhood. While men and women might approach this differently, both genders gain by building faith-based relationships with others. These relationships are valuable in different and deeper ways than your friendly relationships, which also have a place in your life. But Corner 4s, they challenge you. They hold you accountable. They tell you what you need but may not want to hear.

Another source of Corner 4 people is professional peer groups. Vistage, Reboot or Convene are just a few. These organizations all work similarly to be places where its members can safely share even intimate details of their workplaces and get honest, challenging feedback about their leadership. Group sizes tend to be from eight to twelve people. Confidentiality is of utmost importance.

Give Others the Authority to Hold You Accountable

When you give others the authority to hold you accountable, you're taking a big step toward staying out of your own way. Don't overcomplicate this. Getting married or otherwise commiting to a serious relationship can be a source of accountability. Having a pet holds you accountable. Being a coach of a 5th grade basketball team holds you accountable. Having a personal trainer who expects you to be at the fitness center at 6am holds you accountable.

It's tempting to think you don't need this external accountability. Especially if you're wired like me. If you're someone who is a self-starter, who defines your own goals, who gets things done because it's fulfilling the contract you have with yourself, you can easily deny that you need this. This is a blindspot.

Author Gretchen Rubin explains in her book, *The Four Tendencies*, that some people are wired to need the external support structure and some are not. I don't think I need accountability for many of my professional and even some personal objectives because I get stuff done. But that got me into trouble when I focused so much on my professional ambitions and sacrificed many other important parts of my life like faith, church, community, and service.

It's dangerous to not take this seriously. In *The Power of the Other,* Dr. Cloud tells the story of a world-class surgeon who had been repeatedly unfaithful to his wife. The wife finally said she couldn't go on. The surgeon came to Cloud with an impressive, well-thought out plan to repair himself and reclaim his marriage. When he asked Cloud what he thought of the plan Cloud said gave him bad news - he said it would likely fail because it dealt solely with the surgeon's strengths, not his weaknesses. The surgeon's strengths aren't what got him into his troubles - it was his weaknesses. The plan also relied 100% on the surgeon to execute it and comply with it. There was no Corner 4 accountability.

What's Next?

Staying out of your own way is a journey, not a destination. You may repeatedly fall off the rails and have to find your way back.

When you admit you can't travel the journey alone, when you embrace humility and the gift of falling, when you are intentional and unconditional about being vulnerable, you're living a life that makes you a better person and a better sales leader. You'll be a role model to everyone you meet.

Most of us live lives of getting in our own way. We block the path to more fulfilling lives because of our blindspots. Our unflattering habits have become well-worn grooves.

There's something else that influences your coaching effectiveness and that causes blindspots—it's the sales process. While the intentions of sales process are nearly always good, the results are by no means always positive. Let's look at how sales process and the transparency of data can affect your coaching and leadership .

Part 2: Another Cause of Blindspots – Data

6

The Role of Data in Today's Sales Process: A Blessing and a Curse

"Data is the new bacon."
– Seen on a t-shirt

"I'm looking up in the sky and I have no idea which cloud has all my data."
– Unknown

In the preceding section, the notion of blindspots was attributed to factors such as ego, lack of vulnerability and humility, and how you're wired. The paradox of the vice in the virtue reigns large. These are all very personal elements. But blindspots also appear due to another paradox, this one related to data. Too much data can cause you to have blindspots of a different type. In this section you'll learn why this happens and what you can do about it.

If you're like all of my clients, your sales data's "integrity" is suspect. Too much of it is not real. An executive once joked to me that half of his sales pipeline is not real. When I said wow that's a problem he replied "Not really. The problem is not knowing which half is not real."

Your salespeople don't keep their pipelines up to date. They don't always add the new opportunities. They don't move deals when they change sales funnel stages. It makes your job of coaching a lot harder.

To avoid blindspots and effectively coach, you need good data. In one of the early *Diehard* movies, starring the actor Bruce Willis, playing one of the good guys, there's a scene where a plane is trying to land at Washington Dulles airport. The weather is made-for-Hollywood awful, snowy and windy with zero visibility. The plane's low on fuel. They may have only one pass at the landing. If that isn't enough, the big problem is the bad guys took over the control tower and are communicating directly with the pilots and the pilots don't know this.

The main villain says calmly to the pilot, "Windsor 114 you're cleared for ILS approach on runway two niner."

What the pilot doesn't know is that the bad guys recalibrated the network system the pilot is using to gauge the plane's altitude. They've artificially "lowered" sea level by 200 feet. If the pilot's altimeter reading shows 1,000 feet, it really means the plane is at 800 feet, and if the altimeter shows the plane at 200 feet, it means the plane is really at... yes, ground zero. With zero visibility the pilot for Windsor 114 has no way of visually seeing the runway until the last few seconds. Unless Bruce and the good guys act fast, the plane will likely crash and explode upon landing.

Fortunately, having good sales data isn't a life or death issue. But it can make a huge difference in your coaching. In this chapter I'll show you what good data looks like. In the next chapter I'll show you how to get good data to avoid more blindspots.

Defining Data

Since you're focused on generating sales growth I'll limit the definition of good sales data to "net new" business. Net new business is your incremental sales. It's the incremental sales you get when your salesperson closes a new account. It's also the incremental sales that come from existing customers buying more from you. It doesn't matter if net new comes from new customers or from existing customers. It all contributes to growth and growth gets you closer to hitting quota.

For the purpose of this book, I'm using the terms funnel, sales funnel, pipeline, and sales pipeline interchangeably. Let's start with a simple but important definition of the sales funnel:

The sales funnel is simply a list of all of the opportunities or deals that a sales person is actively spending selling time on and has responsibility for.

Sales Funnel Data = Transparency

Business executives have developed a ravenous appetite for data and they're spending big money in capturing it in CRM systems. There's more sales funnel data, opportunity data, account data, win-rate data, activity data, and more than ever before. This data is intended to help executives be smarter and run businesses better. While it might be making some managers smarter, it's not always making them better coaches. Here's why.

More data has created unprecedented transparency of "the work" of the salesperson. Everything salespeople do is exposed. And scrutinized. This new level of exposure often creates tension between manager and seller, which can threaten trust, create defensiveness, and lead to unflattering conversations between the sales manager and salesperson.

For example, routine questioning to a sales manager sometimes feels like an interrogation to the salesperson. During a sales pipeline inspection I've heard sales managers say the following:

- Why is that deal still at stage 1?
- You forecasted these two deals to close last month. Why should

I believe they'll close this month?
- How come you don't have more in your funnel?
- How in the world will you hit quota this quarter with a funnel like that?
- You're not talking to the right people. She's not the decision maker.
- You completed very few of your Goals from last month's 30-day plan.
- You're behind year to date.
- Why don't you have more stage zeros?
- I think you don't have enough Goals defined on your 30-day plan.
- You've been chasing that deal for a long time. Why isn't it moving along?

By the way, one manager asked all of these questions during one call! All of the questions or statements above are reasonable to ask or make. *That's the point.* More data has made it reasonable to ask more questions about deals and funnels. But even when the questions are reasonable to ask, they can put the salesperson on the defensive. When the manager's tone is negative, the salesperson can feel like she's being judged, talked down to, or not appreciated. I've heard conversations that bordered on bullying. In my debrief with the manager, he had no idea he came across that way. Big blindspot. How much learning do you think happens when a salesperson is treated like this?

Don't think I'm suggesting managers not drill down into deals and funnels. I'm saying it's important to have greater self-awareness of how you come across to your salespeople if you want to be a leader who creates emotional connections. Let's connect some dots related to transparency of data:
- More data means more transparency of the work of selling.

- More transparency means more exposure.
- More exposure means more tension between seller and manager.
- More tension means more distrust and defensiveness.
- More distrust means less emotional connection.
- Less emotional connection means the salesperson is less motivated to sell for you.

If you think that these transparency-related blindspots are behaviors that your salespeople need to just laugh off and dismiss, or that salespeople just need to have thicker skins, remember that when good salespeople leave to work for another company, they don't leave their companies as much as they leave their sales managers.

Blessing and Curse

This data transparency is both a blessing and a curse. It's a blessing because it can make sales managers and their salespeople smarter and therefore help them make better decisions regarding selling.

But it can be a curse, too. Because the work is transparent, there's nowhere to hide, so to speak. Everything a salesperson does is seen in the CRM—and is under scrutiny. It is warts and all. If the rep's funnel lacks early stage deals, the manager sees it. If the opportunity data is not updated, the manager sees it. If the call activity records are spotty, he sees it. If win rate is tracked, you can see if she ranks at the bottom. Managers see the deals that haven't moved stages in six months. They see the lack of funnel opportunities for new customers. This transparency-driven scrutiny often creates an atmosphere that is sometimes more like a sparring bout where the manager throws jabs of judgment and the salesperson counters with defensiveness. I've witnessed conversations between managers and reps that are full of tension, doubt, skepticism, lack of trust, accusations, blame, and loads of judgment. Remember, these are supposed to be *coaching* conversations.

When Data Causes Blindspots

This transparency of data causing blindspots must seem strange. So think of it this way: If you found out that something you routinely did, that was generally accepted to be good for you, was suddenly proven to not be good for you, how would you feel? Confused? Conflicted?

Take exercise as an example. Wouldn't it be crazy if health experts discovered that exercise wasn't good for us? How do you think you would react? Deny it? Disagree with it? If you don't exercise, maybe you would feel vindicated!

This probably sounds crazy. Sales data is a good thing, so how can it be a bad thing? Can it be both a good thing and a bad thing? Yes, and that's what makes this dynamic deeply contradictory. It's another vice in the virtue.

To understand the connection between data and blindspots, we need to take a short trip down data lane to see how data has become so paramount in business and sales. But first let's simply define sales data.

Sales Data in CRM Systems

By *data* I'm talking about all that sales information you would typically find in any CRM system. Senior sales leaders, CEOs and owners routinely invest in CRM and subsequently make their sales forces create and capture this data because they believe it will help them run better businesses and deliver results. This data includes:

Opportunity Data
Data about or by:
- Opportunity aging
- Sales cycle time

- Win rate
- Products or services
- Segment
- Geography
- Size
- Margin percentage
- Lead source
- Cost to win opportunities

Sales Funnel (Pipeline) Data:
- Number of opportunities on the sales funnel
- Number of opportunities by stage
- "Turnover" data, sales funnel (pipeline) data
- Funnel value
- Forecasting data
- Number of new opportunities added to the funnel

Account Data:
- Target accounts
- Ideal customer matches
- Demographic account data (SIC code, location, private or public, by sector, etc.)
- Contract or buying group data

Sales Call Data:
- Sales call activity data
- Percent of primary objectives achieved
- Percent of secondary objectives achieved
- Upselling data
- Deal-size data

How and When Did Business Become Obsessed with Data?

It's tempting to think that all this obsession with data is a recent phenomenon. But data capturing has been around for decades, according to a 2013 article, "A Very Short History of Data Science," in *Forbes* magazine by Gil Press, managing partner of a marketing, publishing, research and education consulting company. He traces the topic back to 1944. In 1962, statistician John Tukey wrote, "The Future of Data Analysis," suggesting that the field of statistics was a means to another end, analyzing data and somehow benefiting from that.

In 1977 the International Association for Statistical Computing was created to link traditional statistical methodology, modern computer technology, and the knowledge of domain experts in order to convert data into information and knowledge. In other words (mine), it made it possible for really smart people to use technologies to understand our behaviors better.

A 1994 cover story in *Business Week* magazine dealt with database marketing and how companies were aggressively collecting information on consumers. The intent was to create targeted marketing messages that would influence consumers throughout their buying process. In 1996 the term "data science" was used to headline a major conference, and in 1997 the chair in statistics at the University of Michigan, Jeff Wu, suggested that statistics be called data science.

Over the subsequent two decades attention on data science increased. Hal Varian, Google's chief economist in 2009, is quoted as saying the sexy job of the next decade (yes, the one we're almost through with) will be statisticians, aka data scientists. He said, "The ability to take data—to be able to understand it, to process it, to extract value from it, to communicate it—that's going to be a hugely important skill in the next decade."

You think?

In 2011 author Michael Lewis published the book, *Money Ball*, and gave us an inside look at how data analysis was used by the Oakland Athletics manager Billy Beane, to compete against teams that had payrolls filled with high-priced and very talented players. Beane used the approach to evaluate and identify players he could buy for a lot less than others and who could still help his team win championships.

Every business seems to want data on us. My bank website asks me to allow or not allow my location to the site. Amazon recommends books based on the books I have read. Delta Airlines asks me to take a short survey following a phone experience. In the 2012 U.S. presidential campaign, Barack Obama's campaign manager, Jim Messina, is quoted as saying, "We are going to measure everything." They employed data scientists that ran computer simulations to get insights that were used in campaign strategy.

I had a funny, data experience years ago while in Bangkok, Thailand on business. I had just cleared customs and was immediately given the chance to score my experience by selecting one of five facial expressions that appeared on a touch screen. A big smile meant I was delighted, and a frown meant I wasn't too happy with it. Moments later I had another chance to use the same system to score my level of satisfaction with my experience in the toilet. Too much information.

Data in Sales

The data evolution in sales coincided with the growth of CRM systems. ACT! and Goldmine were early software companies in the 1980s that targeted the sales function. Tom Siebel left Oracle in the early 1990s and started Siebel Systems, to create what was called a "sales force automation" product (SFA). SFA became CRM, "customer relationship management." Bigger players entered the market with products. Salesforce.com emerged with a SaaS offering, software as a service, in 1999 and now is one of the top providers in the world.

The crush of strong economic growth coming out of the Great

Blindspots: The Hidden Killer of Sales Coaching

Recession in 2008 through today in 2019 has driven the growth of data capture and analysis. Senior leaders of companies including CFOs, COOs, and CMOs, not just heads of salesforces, want more data for many reasons including:

- The need to forecast more accurately
- Prevent tribal knowledge from leaving the company when a sales person leaves
- Help with strategic planning
- Impact sales funnel management
- Drive more leads through nurturing campaigns
- Qualify leads better by scoring them
- Know when to hand off leads to sales from marketing, business development, or customer service
- Better utilize selling resources by understanding customer buying journey
- Improve productivity of field sales teams
- Design more effective coverage maps
- Impact go-to-market strategies

Some companies are making impressive strides toward capturing and acting on sales data. Often, they have made the necessary people investments such as administrative assistants for salespeople or sales operations staff and data analytics experts. In a 2016 survey of 1000 sales organizations, McKinsey & Company found that 53% of the companies that McKinsey considered high-performing rated themselves as effective users of analytics.

It's common to see other companies struggle with their data efforts. Getting salespeople to enter and update CRM is a constant battle. Their sales funnels have outdated close dates and stage data. Forecasting is still a good measure of art versus science. Marketing isn't always sure that leads have been properly followed up. CRM can be the elephant in the room that no one wants to mention. What executive wants to acknowledge that the six-figure investment he signed off on is not producing the tangible results he expected?

In the same McKinsey survey, they found that 57% of sales organizations did not view themselves as effective users of advanced analytics. So, while getting more data is the directive, there's still a big gap in effectively using it.

Blindspots from Data

Okay, enough about the history of data science. What does a blindspot due to data actually look like?

Let me tell you about a Funnel Audit conversation I coached between a sales manager and her salesperson.

While the manager did a good job of analyzing the salesperson's funnel, something interesting happened at the beginning of the call. The salesperson seemed excited about the health of his funnel. The data showed positive trends in certain leading indicators. The manager made a few comments. Then, the salesperson shut down. He went from talkative and excited to quiet. The contrast was obvious to me. His replies to the manager's questions, when the manager stopped to ask one, were short. It was clear to me that she missed this change in demeanor.

Later I learned that the positive trends in the health of the funnel were the outcomes of the salesperson taking the manager's previous coaching seriously to improve his funnel health. Now he was proud of the progress, like a cat dropping a dead mouse at the owner's feet, but the manager had made it a buzz kill by not recognizing the progress.

I debriefed with the manager to get her impression without revealing my observations. She thought it went well, but she commented that she's still frustrated, struggling to get this rep to work the sales process. "What do I need to do?" she asked me.

I shared with the manager my observations of the rep's change in demeanor and suggested it could be due to not getting recognized by the manager. She didn't notice it, but she did say she felt bad because this was something she had been working on.

Think about this for a second. It's one thing that a manager's recognition meter is low, but even in light of trying to improve on it, she can't. That's how powerful these blindspots can be.

Here's the punch line to the data transparency issue—I asked her if she knew why she didn't notice the change in the rep's demeanor. She said she was focused on the data and the process. She completely missedthe cues he was giving. What could have been a really powerful call became another coaching opportunity hijacked by a blindspot.

By the end of the week I got a message from the manager that she had called the rep and apologized for not recognizing the strides he had made in taking her coaching. That took humility. I was very proud of her.

More Blindspots from Data

Blindspots from data can affect sales opportunity discussions. CRM makes it easy to pull up information about opportunities, but what's often missing is a flow framework for the conversation. The manager ends up firing lots of questions and the rep often gets defensive. I joined this call between a manager and his salesperson. Here's how the dialogue went. Note: PFA stands for Person with Financial Authority, a key influencer in the customer's buying journey:

Manager: Why hasn't Star Industries moved stages? Seems like it's not moved for months.
Salesperson: It's actually a stage 2 now.

Manager: Your CRM says stage 1. And $50,000 doesn't seem right.

Salesperson: I know I need to update it. And it's more like $200,000 when you include the installation and set up.

Manager: I don't know why you wouldn't have this updated. How many other deals on your pipeline need to be updated in CRM? Seems like we've been talking about this opportunity forever.

Salesperson: I've been meeting with Sheila Richards. She's really busy. She knows she needs to do something. The unit's not working like it should.

Manager: Is she the PFA?

Salesperson: She's the one who would bring it up. She's got experience with these kinds of problems and has a lot of credibility. And I've got a history with her.

Manager: But who's the PFA? If you don't get to the PFA, how is it going to move?

Salesperson: Her boss is probably the PFA.

Manager: Why aren't you trying to see him?

Salesperson: If you think seeing Sheila is hard, seeing him is next to impossible. And I've been running around taking care of a lot of other fires and haven't had time. They're up to their necks with a LEAN project that's taking everyone's time.

Manager: Who is it? What's his name? The PFA...

Salesperson: Ken Miller, he's the Vice President of Operations.

Manager: She knows she needs to do something. What's the problem? Why isn't it a priority? Have you had that conversation with Sheila?

Salesperson: She wants to, she's told me that. She probably needs a little time.

Manager: Time isn't likely to change anything but having a compelling problem that's causing heartburn is. Does she have enough heartburn?

Blindspots: The Hidden Killer of Sales Coaching

Salesperson: I don't know.

Manager: You need to get Sheila to commit to getting us a meeting with Ken Miller. I'd like to be at that meeting. He might respond better to someone at his level.

Salesperson: I'll reach out to her.

Can you sense the tone of the manager? He sounds impatient, doesn't he? He's searching for important answers to reasonable questions that the salesperson needs to know or be asking himself, but it borders on interrogation. He uses several 'why' questions which can be sharp edged. Did you notice the salesperson's responses early were more elaborate than responses later in the dialogue?

I don't intend to come off as overly critical of the manager. To be fair to him, and to you sales managers, the job these days has an increased administrative and reporting obligation, again, due to the increased possibilities that CRM brings. What sometimes gets sacrificed is time spent coaching. It's tempting to cut to the chase during opportunity discussions, to fill your gap in knowledge. And with some salespeople who aren't as talkative you're going to have to lead the conversation more.

Why Does Sales Data Cause Blindspots for Sales Managers?

1. More data means the work of selling is more transparent.

To be transparent means to be easily visible. Conspicuous. Transparency of sales data means you can see "the work of selling," literally, the input of what a salesperson does on any given day, in any given week. But it also removes a salesperson's cover, leaving them exposed to your impressions, conclusions and judgments based on that data.

For example, go into a salesperson's CRM account and you'll see if her sales funnel is healthy or sick and more, such as:

- The aging of the deals on her sales funnel
- If she has any deals that are well past the average cycle time for a deal
- Her call activity
- When she updates CRM. Is it batched, is it updated the night before it's due, or does she regularly update it
- Her win rate
- How many leads she's closed from the marketing campaigns
- What share of customers she's penetrating
- If she leans mostly toward selling one product or line of business or if she sells across multiple lines

The data is a window into the salesperson's efforts and skills. For example, if Mary's funnel has stalled opportunities, the manager might conclude Mary's not putting in the effort to move them, or she's not skilled at getting to the right stakeholders, or she doesn't take the manager's coaching, or even that she doesn't care. Sometimes these conclusions can be right and sometimes they can be way off. Once a manager is presented with a pattern of data, the biases he has about the rep could be impossible to overcome. He puts her in the box and thinks he has her figured out. This can lead to little or no coaching at all.

2. Transparency doesn't tell the whole story.

An irony of transparency is that it tempts you to think you're getting the full story of each of your reps and how they go about their job. More sales data might be like the results of your blood work from an annual physical exam. The chart shows a person who is overweight and has high blood pressure, but it doesn't show how he got there. Is it hereditary or is it diet? Maybe there's no exercise to be found. This background leads to a better diagnosis and treatment. A sales manager discovers the full story by carefully doing what Leanne did with Michael - she made time to get to know him. Bert didn't.

3. Deal discussions are more like interrogations.

Unfortunately, with greater transparency, sales managers have more ammunition to fire away with questions. More transparency means managers are tempted to believe they already have the answers in front of them: Your funnel sucks. You can't prospect at all. You can't close the deals at lower funnel stages. What more do I need to know? It's tempting to race through deal discussions.

Transparency creates tension and that makes deal and sales funnel conversations more complicated. The intent of the purposeful sales manager in asking all of these reasonable questions is good—which makes the blindspot even bigger. The manager just wants to help but instead the questionning wears down the salesperson.

One thing I've seen good managers do to avoid coming off like an interrogation is to reinforce and remind the salesperson of the process. For example, the manager will say prior to a deal review, "Before we get started is there anything you want me to do or not to do?" He might add, "I've got a lot of questions around this deal but I come off as interrogating you don't hesitate to call a time out, ok?"

4. What is routine gets taken for granted.

If you think of any event you routinely engage in, be it personal or business related, there's always the risk of taking it for granted. The same can happen for routine or regular coaching conversations.

At the beginning of our Funnel Audits good managers will say something like, "As a reminder, even though we do these every month I want to make sure you're getting value from today's conversation. What do you think we need to focus on regarding your funnel right now?" They might add later in the conversation "I don't want my comments around your 30 day plan to sound like nitpicking or wordsmithing so if you disagree with a comment don't hesitate to let me know."

One way our clients battle the routine of Funnel Audit conversations is to make sure they take into consideration where they are in the fiscal year. This is important to managing one's funnel. Let's consider a business where the sales cycles average 4-6 months. In Q1 salespeople are trying to get a fast start and build some early funnel health. By Q2 they're deep into building a healthy funnel that will produce revenue by midyear and the back half of the year. In the middle of the year there's this feeling of halftime and needing a strong second half to hit quota. Then, in the last quarter it is the final stretch. The focus is to close what you can to impact the year. There's not much funnel building that can go on in Q4 that will still become this year's sales. At each of these periods the salesperson should be thinking differently about his funnel and therefore the conversations you have with your salespeople need to be different. Your job as sales manager is to provide context around those periods. This helps the salesperson prevent a feeling of routine.

5. Your salesperson doesn't get any value from coaching conversations.

I coach my managers to constantly question the value they are providing to their teams. This helps avoid settling into the mindset of 'we're doing 'x' because we've always done 'x'. For example, a Funnel Audit every 30 days sounds valuable, but not if the salesperson gets little from them. If he sees it as an exercise benefiting his manager, not him, these conversations will eventually break down. If deal reviews lack structure, go on too long, and feel like an interrogation, they won't add much value. Unfortunately, what passes as coaching is sometimes just telling by the sales manager. If there's a low level of self-awareness the manager has no idea how he or she comes across. The manager can be confused as to why the rep isn't responding to her coaching or his feedback. Remember, you have a right by your title to manage your salespeople but the title doesn't give you the right to coach them. You have to earn that.

6. The salesperson doesn't respect the manager.

If you've ever had a manager you didn't respect, you probably struggled to take his or her coaching seriously, or even to stay motivated. There was probably no emotional connection. Sometimes the lack of respect is due to a personality clash. If the salesperson has a big personality that struggles to be emotionally vulnerable to anyone, and the manager is someone who likes to get very personal with his reps, they may not connect. Or, if the manager is very clean, tidy and organized and the rep is scattered and disorganized, and she gets pounded for that, she'll struggle to emotionally connect with the manager.

Sometimes the lack of respect is related to a senior or veteran salesperson who now has a much younger, maybe less experienced sales manager. If you're the younger manager, you'll want to work on developing more credibility with these veteran salespeople. One way to do that is to spend time with them observing and learning. Ask them questions about the business and the market. Consider inviting them into region meeting training events or to be a resource for others in the region. I also suggest not trying to beat them at their game of more years and experience than you. That's a losing battle. For instance, instead of trying to become as smart as your rep in the product or application, turn your attention to helping with things where you can add more value like territory management, defining priorities, making presentations, sales funnel management or even negotiation skills.

Data Driven Blindspots Need Not Sink You

Blindspots from data is primarily an issue of transparency, which has raised the level of tension for every sales manager and salesperson I've met. It's a paradox. It's a blessing and a curse. You know from earlier chapters that blindspots need to be dealt with or else they steadily erode your coaching and leadership effectiveness.

Data's not going away. But data isn't the enemy, like money isn't the root of evil. Realize that more data does not automatically lead to better coaching and leadership. You'll have to learn to not only leverage data to be a better coach but also expertly manage the downsides of more data.

In the next chapter you'll learn how our clients organize the data around their sales funnels to communicate more clearly, set better priorities and hold everyone accountable.

7

The Need for Good Sales Data

"If you're a scientist and you have to have an answer,
even in the absence of data, you're not going to be
a good scientist."
– Neil deGrasse Tyson, Astrophysicist

It goes without saying that you need good, accurate sales data to coach effectively. Without good data it might be like giving someone the right directions to the wrong place.

One of the things that could get in the way of good data is not having a clear way of talking about it or not having the data organized in a logical, easy to use manner.

I'd like to share with you some ways of organizing sales funnel data that will improve communication between you and your salespeople and help you more quickly understand the health of a sales funnel. This will save you time and make your coaching more impactful. You'll learn about the tools that our clients use to do this.

Accuracy Counts

Good sales data around net new business simply means that what the salesperson reports or documents regarding value of the funnel, opportunity size, number of opportunities per stage, the stage of each opportunity, etc. is accurate. For example, if Mary in territory 101 says she has a $3M sales funnel, then good data means it's really a $3M sales funnel. If she says she has three deals in progress at stage 2, none at stage 3, nine deals at stage 4, two deals at stage 5, and none at stage 6, then good data means that the deals really are where she says they are in the customer buying journey. And if she tells her sales manager she's forecasting $475,000 to close in the next 30 days, then good data means that's really going to happen.

In reality, Mary's reporting on her funnel isn't always 100% accurate. Sometimes she overstates her funnel value by including deals that shouldn't be counted as funnel value yet. Sometimes she forgets to add the new sales opportunities she uncovers from week to week. Sometimes she says she's got four deals that are likely to close in the month, but she closes only one. Her funnel very likely has some bad data on it.

I've seen just about every version of bad sales data you can imagine. Maybe you've seen your share too. If it makes you feel better, it's highly likely that every salesperson in every company has some degree of bad sales data around opportunities and the sales funnel.

The $36 Million Funnel

To highlight the consequences of bad data I share with you a situation that occurred many years ago with one of my company's first large scale implementations of The Funnel Principle. It was a crucial test of our process.

As we always do when we first work with a new client, we started by co-creating with the client a custom BuyCycle Funnel™ model (I'll talk more about this in the next chapter) for their business. This model defines the client's customer's buying journey. It's a foundation that everything else in the sales process is built on. Before going live with it and training all of the salespeople in it we asked one of the regional sales managers, I'll call Dave, to do a "before and after" exercise, in this case for just one of the five product segments they sold. We asked him to determine the value of his region funnel using his current funnel model (before) and then determine the value of the funnel after applying the BuyCycle Funnel™ model (after). Again, this was for just one product segment.

The "before" funnel value was $36M. The "after" funnel value was $5.6M. How did that happen? Dave's salespeople had placed most of their opportunities on their funnels at the wrong stages and put many of them further along the customer journey than they really were. You'll see in detail in the next chapter how this happened. For now let's stay on the point of the need to have good data. After Dave recovered from the shock and anger, we discussed how this affected his coaching.

Data Drives Behavior

Remember how the pilots flying the *Die Hard* plane flew thought that the altimeter data was correct? Of course they would. Their behavior, how they flew the plane, was based on the data. Similarly, *data drives your sales coaching behavior*. Thinking he had a $36M dollar funnel, Dave did what any good manager would do—he coached to it. Data said he had a $36M funnel chasing a $1.8M quota for the one segment. That sounds pretty good doesn't it? He coached his reps to close what was already on their funnels.

If Dave's region had closed even 20% of their funnel opportunities, that would have been directionally worth about $7.2M, a number a lot higher than the $1.8M quota he was chasing. Ka-ching! He would have blown away his quota for that segment.

Unfortunately, Dave's coaching was not going to work because the data was wrong. There wasn't enough there. $36M was really $5.6M. Using the same 20% close rate for this $5.6M funnel, that strategy would yield directionally about $1.12M of new sales, not the $7.2M he thought he would get. And it wouldn't be enough to hit the $1.8M quota. In fact, that's what eventually happened. Dave's region didn't hit its quota for this segment for the year.

Another way of looking at it is Dave's coaching was not aligned with the sales funnel health. Their funnels needed more opportunities on them. And specifically, more opportunities that could be counted as funnel value. That meant his entire team should have been moving the early stage funnel opportunities to mid or late stages, instead of focusing heavily on closing mid- and late-stage deals that weren't really at mid and late stages. A lot of time was spent executing on the wrong priorities. Over a region, that inefficiency adds up. Over multiple regions, it's even worse.

How should Dave have coached to a $5.6M funnel?

First, he should have made a regular habit of inspecting his reps' funnels. Instead, they were all taken by surprise later when they discovered their funnels were off track. And by then it was too late to make sick funnels healthy. Funnel inspections are more than just talking about the funnel. Dave talked about it too. But he didn't talk about the funnel the right way.

Second, with good data Dave would have helped each rep align their priorities to the health of their specific funnel. If we just assume that most of the salespeople had funnels that were not big enough, the priority would be to make the funnels bigger. This might sound simple but that doesn't mean Dave should have just shouted louder, "Go get more in your funnel!" He needed to translate that simple direction into specific, unique objectives and actions for each salesperson. For example, for one salesperson it might mean making upselling a priority. For another salesperson it might mean getting new customers. For another it might mean focusing on pull through from an established base.

In addition to needing good data it helps to have a way to discuss funnel health and opportunities with your salespeople. In this next section let's see the language our clients use to do this.

A Sample Funnel

Let's pretend you're a sales manager and Carly is one of your salespeople. Let's analyze Carly's funnel using The Funnel Principle and use a simple 3-stage customer buying journey model for this exercise. We don't consider "closed" to be a buying-journey stage. Closed means a funnel opportunity is no longer on the funnel—you've received a contract or purchase order.

A Simple 3-Stage Customer Buying Journey Model

Early Stage: the customer has expressed interest and shared the pain, but hasn't committed to making a change or a purchase.

Mid Stage: the customer has committed to making a purchase but not necessarily from your company. The pain is compelling enough to do something about it.

Late Stage: the customer is one step from making the purchase, but again not necessarily from you.

Let's say Carly's funnel looks like this:

Early Stage: She has two deals totaling $50,000

Mid Stage: She has 14 deals totaling $750,000

Late Stage: She has one deal totaling $65,000

Let me add that it's July 3 and Carly is halfway through the year that ends December 31. She's got a $1M quota and her YTD (year to date) sales is $600,000. To simplify the example let's say that any sale she makes within the year is booked 100% of the value of the sale. For example, if she closes a $75,000 sale on December 22, that $75,000 sale value is booked 100% toward this year's quota.

Funnel Dashboard

Carly will benefit from having a way to quickly see some important information about her sales funnel. A convenient and common way to show her funnel information is with a dashboard like the one below. Funnel dashboards are good visuals for quick information and they save you and the salesperson a lot of time when you discuss the funnel health. So far, we know this about Carly's funnel:

Quota	$1,000,000
YTD sales	$ 600,000
Quota gap	$ 400,000

So, there's really just one question to ask: Is Carly's funnel healthy enough to close another $400,000 of sales by year end? One step to answering that is to know how much TVR her funnel has.

TVR – An Honest Measure of Funnel Value

TVR stands for Total Viable Revenue. I introduced the term 16 years ago and wrote about it in my book *The Funnel Principle*. Here's the definition:

> **TVR is the total value (dollar, euro, etc.) of all of the sales opportunities that have reached or passed the stage where the customer is committed to buying something from someone.**

In this simple 3-stage funnel TVR is the sum total of all opportunities at the Mid and Late stages.

Salespeople may not always know with high certainty that a deal has reached this TVR phase, even when they ask good questions. However, too many times they don't know because they're not asking good questions, or any questions at all.

Using TVR as a concept is another way of defining how qualified the sales opportunity is. I've learned that too often salespeople tend to see opportunities as more qualified than they really are, meaning they're further along the customer buying journey. That results in deals being counted as TVR that shouldn't be. Like in Dave's $36M funnel. For many of the opportunities on his region funnel, the salespeople had not disqualified the customer's commitment to buy something from someone. All of this led to bad data.

To be clear, once a sales opportunity reaches Mid stage on this simple 3-stage funnel, it is considered TVR. Carly needs to add up the deal value for all deals that are at Mid and Late stages to calculate TVR. Early stage opportunities are not counted in TVR.

Let's add the following information to Carly's Funnel Dashboard:

Quota	$1,000,000
YTD sales	$ 600,000
Quota gap	$ 400,000
TVR	$ 815,000

Now do we know if this funnel is healthy enough to hit the quota? Is $815,000 of TVR enough to close the quota gap and hit quota? We need a little more information. We need to know what win rate Carly uses. This leads to our next three terms.

Win Rate, Funnel Factor and Target TVR

Win rate is simply this:

**Number of deals closed/Number of deals
actively pursued = Win rate**

For example, if you close five deals and you pursued ten, then your win rate is 5/10 or 50%. If you close three deals and you pursued ten then your win rate is 30%.

The Funnel Factor is a fixed number that the salesperson "manages her funnel to." Funnel Factor is calculated by the following formula:

1/win rate percentage = Funnel Factor

For example, if you believe Carly has a 50% hit rate on TVR deals, then the Funnel Factor would be 2. You get this by dividing 1 by the win rate.

1/50% = 2

This means you would help Carly manage her funnel to a factor of 2. Knowing win rate is important to funnel management. If you misjudge the win rate even by a little bit, it could have significant impact on your productivity and sales. For example, if you think your win rate is 50% when it's really 33%, you're not overestimating your win rate by 17%, you're overestimating it by 51%!

This Funnel Factor is used to determine how big Carly's sales funnel should be or how much TVR it should have as you'll see next.

Target TVR

Target TVR is how big Carly's funnel needs to be for her to feel confident that she can close another $400,000 of sales to hit her quota. The formula for Target TVR is:

Target TVR = quota gap X Funnel Factor

Carly's quota gap is $400,000. With a 50% win rate, the Funnel Factor is 2. Therefore, her Target TVR is $800,000. Now the Funnel dashboard looks like this:

Blindspots: The Hidden Killer of Sales Coaching

Quota	$1,000,000
YTD sales	$ 600,000
Quota gap	$ 400,000
Target TVR	$ 800,000
TVR	$ 815,000

It's looking good, right? She has slightly more TVR ($815,000) than Target TVR ($800,000). Time to celebrate right? If Carly's funnel has good data, then we certainly like her chances of hitting quota. Her manager's coaching should focus on winning the TVR deals, not adding a lot more TVR to her funnel. But proceed with caution.

What If Carly's Funnel Isn't Accurate?

Too often the reported TVR number is incorrectly too high, making the funnel look healthier than it really is. This is usually due to the salesperson placing the opportunities at the wrong funnel stages. Let's say that we ask Carly a few questions about her funnel and soon get the impression that her TVR is not accurate. Let's say we find that she has put early stage opportunities at the mid or late stages of her funnel, thereby artificially inflating TVR. We inspect her funnel (a Funnel Audit) to help Carly put the opportunities at the right stages. As a result, several of her Mid stage opportunities get moved back to Early stage. This makes her TVR smaller.

Next is the before data that is bad (before our Funnel Audit with Carly) and the after data that is good.

Before		After
Early Stage	50,000	325,000
Mid Stage	750,000	475,000
Late Stage	65,000	65,000

The revised funnel dashboard now looks like this:

Quota	$1,000,000
YTD sales	$ 600,000
Quota gap	$ 400,000
Target TVR	$ 800,000
TVR	$ 540,000

Now the funnel doesn't have enough TVR. That leads us to another term called TVR Shortfall. TVR Shortfall is the additional amount of TVR that the funnel needs in order to be at Target TVR. Now Carly's dashboard looks like this:

Quota	$1,000,000
YTD sales	$ 600,000
Quota gap	$ 400,000
Target TVR	$ 800,000
TVR	$ 540,000
TVR Shortfall	$ 260,000

Carly's funnel has a TVR Shortfall of $260,000. If she doesn't eliminate this TVR Shortfall, then we have less confidence that she'll hit her quota. There is one way she could hit her quota with less TVR. Can you think of how that is possible? I'll give you the answer at the end of this chapter.

Now let's compare the recommended coaching with good data (after) to the coaching using the bad data (before).

Bad Data (Before) Funnel Coaching

The funnel with the bad data—showing a TVR of $815,000 and no TVR Shortfall—encourages you to direct Carly to focus more on moving the TVR deals along and closing the 50% that she historically wins. You might want to coach Carly to focus first on the TVR deals that are higher priority, such as the deals that she feels a lot more confident in winning.

Blindspots: The Hidden Killer of Sales Coaching

Maybe those are the deals where she's got solid contacts like coaches or advocates that are helping her. The next priority might be working to advance the other TVR deals. Finally, you might coach her to devote a little time to getting more TVR but not a lot.

If you like time budgets for managing time, you could reasonably coach Carly to spend 70% of her time moving and closing the mid- and late-stage TVR deals and spending 30% of her time moving early stage to TVR stage.

Again and unfortunately, because this is bad data this coaching is misdirected and not very helpful.

After (Good Data) Funnel Coaching

The funnel with the good data shows a TVR Shortfall of $260,000. You should coach Carly to see that her priority is to get more TVR. The first place to go to get more TVR is the early stage deals. There's $325,000 in that bucket. Moving all of the early stage deals to TVR would eliminate the TVR Shortfall. But there's no guarantee that this will happen. Maybe you help Carly focus first on the early stage deals that are higher priority, such as the deals where the product fit might be better, or deals where she has advocates who will help her.

Though she has a TVR Shortfall, she also has TVR that needs to advance to close. The second priority is to advance these TVR deals. Either close them or move them closer to closing.

Carly's time budget between TVR and early stage deals might be somewhat reversed from the bad data funnel. You might advise her to spend 70% of her time trying to move early stage deals to TVR and spend 30% of her time moving TVR deals to close. You can see this coaching is a big difference from the bad data funnel.

The consequence of committing to the wrong priorities and time budgets across TVR and early stage deals is that Carly runs a higher risk of not hitting quota because she won't have enough TVR to become sales before the end of the year. For sales forces that have no disciplined funnel management process like this one, this often results in an "oh shit" moment because it's too late to do anything about it. Instead, having a TVR leading indicator that alerts her to insufficient funnel value lets her take corrective action now and avoid the year-end unpleasant surprise.

Impact of Scale

If one sales rep has bad data on her funnel, the impact to your sales region may be minimal. But if Carly's funnel has bad data, it's likely that other reps in your region have some bad funnel data too.

In the above example there's a delta of $275,000 in TVR—from the bad data example to the good data example. The bad data shows a surplus TVR of $15,000 while the good data shows a TVR Shortfall of $260,000.

Let's say you have eight reps in your region and all have misrepresented the TVR health by the same amount. Your region TVR is inflated by $2.2M. Think of how that will impact your coaching effectiveness, your forecasting and your sales.

How to Prevent Bad Data

It might not be clear yet how you prevent the bad data from getting there in the first place. Simply having funnel dashboards and inspections and TVR and TVR Shortfall information is not enough. The most effective way to prevent bad data on sales funnels is to make sure you have a customer buying journey model (funnel stages) that is designed the right way. In other words, a BuyCycle Funnel™ model. Let's learn about that next.

The answer to the question earlier in the chapter: How can a funnel with a TVR Shortfall still hit quota? The win rate has to increase. Carly

Blindspots: The Hidden Killer of Sales Coaching

would need to close 74% of the $540,000 TVR to give her $400,000 in sales.

8

The Key to Getting Good Sales Data: The BuyCycle Funnel™

"You turned the funnel upside down."
– Gerhard Gschwandtner, publisher of
Selling Power magazine

Introducing the Customer Buying Process

In 2008 a central theme of the Sales 2.0 conference in San Francisco was the "customer buying process." Speaker after speaker presented ideas on how to influence buying at each stage of the customer buying process. This was a dramatic shift in sales thinking. For decades most sales training methods did not put the customer buying process front and center. They didn't teach salespeople to understand how their customers buy from them.

I was invited by Gerhard Gschwandtner to present the customer buying process model for selling that I created in 2000, called the BuyCycle Funnel model. For several years leading up to that conference I had created custom BuyCycle Funnel models for many clients. Their results validated the relevance of this model. I eventually wrote a book about the model and my client experience called *The Funnel Principle.*

Today the concept of selling to the customer's buying process is the new standard. Popular phrases now are "the buying journey," "the buyer journey," and I've recently heard "the consumer decision journey." All of these phrases aim to describe what I introduced 18 years ago—the customer buying process. It thrills me that today I'm not the only one touting the importance of this concept. Well known sales training and research firms have joined the party. At an annual sales and marketing conference, CEB Gartner (The Challenger Sale) principal executive advisor, Brent Adamson, devoted his entire opening speech to the need to sell the way your customers buy.

In addition, Aberdeen Consulting Group reported that companies with formal stage definitions defined by the customer buying process had 33% more accurate sales forecasting and 40% more salespeople making quota. CSO Insights reported that defining how customers buy must be the first place executives begin when conducting sales transformation efforts. I'm thrilled because of the results I've seen the past 18 years with my clients using the BuyCycle Funnel model to impact their businesses. Every company should be designing their sales processes and providing training that is based on how their customers buy from them.

My Inspiration for the BuyCycle Funnel

I had become intrigued with this line of thought nearly a decade before that Selling Power conference. In early 2000 I had begun noodling ideas for a sales model that would help salespeople be more effective. I had a BFO —blinding flash of the obvious—that sounded like this:

**When people make a purchase,
they don't go through a sales process,
they go through a buying process.**

I spent a few years of mental grinding to understand what this meant, and eventually created the BuyCycle Funnel™ model of selling. This model defines how your customers buy from you. It impacts everything about "opportunity management" and the sales funnel. It helps salespeople create better strategies for winning sales opportunities and helps them better manage their overall sales funnels. It delivers good data to the sales funnel.

The Traditional Sales Model

Before I present the BuyCycle Funnel Model let me deconstruct what it replaced. I call that the traditional funnel model.

The traditional funnel model is 100% focused on the seller's activity. Doing demos, making sales calls, setting up trials, dropping off samples, doing a needs analysis, estimating the job, doing an energy audit, preparing a quote or proposal, hosting a site visit, re-quoting a job, delivering or presenting a proposal, etc. are all examples of selling activity. Below is an example of the stages of a traditional funnel.

Traditional Funnel Model

Stage	Sales Stage
1	Initial call
2	Uncover pain and present our capabilities
3	Prepare a proposal or a quote
4	Deliver or present the proposal
5	Negotiate terms and conditions
6	Close the sale
7	Closed

Blindspots: The Hidden Killer of Sales Coaching

Of course you have to do these things in selling! But here's the problem: The selling activity that the salesperson has completed determines the stage. For example, when he sends a proposal, then it's at the proposal stage. But just because he's sent a proposal doesn't mean the customer is ready to act on it. It doesn't even mean the customer has committed to *buying something from someone*. But by proposing something, it's tempting to think the customer is committed and even ready. You can probably think of many examples of your people doing this.

Another example I hear a lot is leaving samples or doing demos. Both selling activities can be valuable. And both can be a major time drain. Perhaps you know salespeople who have done lots of demos and sold little, or who sample everyone and haven't sold much.

Back to the proposal activity, since it's proposed, the salesperson thinks forward to his next selling activity, maybe a big presentation to try to close the sale. Or worse. They wait for the phone to ring with an order. But if that stage 4 opportunity is really a stage 1, then doing later stage selling activities won't have much influence on the sale. In fact, the customer could conclude that the salesperson is really clueless, not listening, or just trying to sell something.

This mistake happens every day in selling. Managers struggle to understand later why a stage 6 deal doesn't close, or why a funnel full of stage 4 and 5 deals is not big enough to close the quota gap. Bad data is the culprit. Using a traditional funnel is often the cause.

The BuyCycle Funnel™ Model

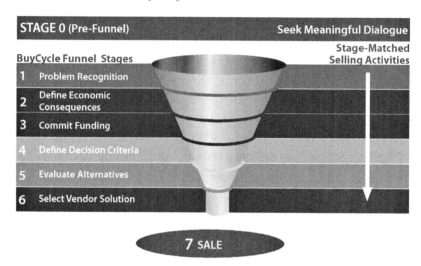

The BuyCycle Funnel Model is a sales model that defines the collective sequence of commitments that customers make when they buy something. The sequence begins at problem or opportunity recognition (Stage 1) and concludes with a purchase (closed). It breaks down the sequence into buying stages. Each stage represents a part of the journey the customer is on. Here's the first key feature of the BuyCycle Funnel model:

> **Sales opportunities are placed at stages based on where the customer is in the buying process, not based on a selling activity the salesperson has completed.**

Knowing where the customer is in their buying process helps the salesperson determine what selling activities he or she should do next to try to influence the customer. This forces the seller to ask and learn instead of traditional show and tell. It helps the seller understand the needs and timing more thoroughly. It helps them uncover stakeholders other than the one they are currently talking to. It shifts the selling focus away from the salesperson's next steps and toward the customer's next steps or commitments.

By contrast, in traditional sales funnel models or sales process models, the stages are defined by seller activity such as doing a demo or giving the customer a proposal. Here's the next key feature of the BuyCycle Funnel model:

> **Customer commitment is what defines deal movement, not selling activity. By defining the buying stages by customer commitments, salespeople can define better sales strategies to move the opportunity along to the next stage.**

This is huge. A selling activity doesn't create deal movement—a customer commitment creates deal movement. A salesperson using a traditional funnel model will think movement has occurred after she completes a selling activity, regardless of any customer response. Here's the third key feature of the BuyCycle Funnel model:

> **Customer buying stages have matching selling activity stages. This way, selling activity is aligned with the customer buying process.**

Instead of being misled by just being busy, managers now have a way to confirm and coach the salesperson to be effective. The customer's buying stage determines the selling activity and strategy. It's logical. It's effective. Here's the fourth key feature:

> **The BuyCycle Funnel™ has two unique stages. The first is a stage that describes the customer as being committed to buying something from someone—if not from you. This stage is pivotal. The second unique stage defines the business impact of the problem.**

Regarding the 'commit to buy from someone' stage, we were skeptical that this might not be relevant for all clients. But 120 clients in the funnel model design workshop confirmed that it's entirely relevant for their business. Regarding the business-impact stage, we learned that B2B customers routinely use this stage not only to justify a spend but to prioritize it. Customers are more likely to decide to buy something from someone when the problem is compelling enough to fix.

Buying Exercise

Go ahead and test the model with a recent, important personal purchase you made or are in the process of making, perhaps something like the following: a piece of furniture for your house or apartment, a remodeling project in your home, a new home or a new car, a vacation, an electronic device like a computer or tablet, an expensive item for a serious hobby like golf clubs or photography, or even a pet.

Whether or not you realized it (most people don't), you went through a buying journey that can be documented using the BuyCycle Funnel model. Now here's the most important question to ask: If a salesperson was involved in your purchase, did he or she make a difference? If yes, at what stages of your buying process did the salesperson influence? How did he or she do that?

If the salesperson didn't help, what didn't he or she do? Did he try to force you to buy when you weren't ready? Did he not add value in educating you? Did she not help you avoid making mistakes like picking the wrong model or size?

Now ask yourself another very important question: How much influence are your salespeople having on your customers when they buy? At what stages of your customer's buying process are your salespeople influencing? If you struggle to answer this, consider it a breakthrough. Now you must do something about it.

Blindspots: The Hidden Killer of Sales Coaching

57% of the Buying Process Is Already Done

The CEB, Corporate Executive Board (now called CEB Gartner), coined the term '57%' after the publishing of its first book, *The Challenger Sale*. They said they had data that showed that customers, on average, went through 57% of their buying process by the time they called a salesperson.

I like the simplicity and shock value of this term, but many people can't translate it to action. It feels intuitively spot on, but what are you going to coach your salespeople to do differently now? There's no reference for that. But the BuyCycle Funnel clarifies it. In my seminars, I ask at what stage does 57% seem like in the BuyCycle Funnel. People almost always say either stage 3 or 4. This means that customers on average have committed funding, Stage 3, or defined the decision criteria, Stage 4, before calling the salesperson. With this clarity you can now coach your salespeople to ask specific questions and to engage in specific selling activities that are relevant to 57%. To start, with 'committing funding' such a pivotal stage in the customer's buying journey your salespeople need to validate that that has happened. Maybe it doesn't surprise you when I say in our experience validation is replaced with assumption.

Buying Process Is Emotional

A customer buying process model might make selling appear to be 100% logical and rational. But we know that's not true. Sales is only part science and human emotions often play a part in the selection process.

I bought a new set of golf clubs three years ago. For ten years before that I had considered, off and on, buying a new set but didn't. Why? I wasn't playing much because my family gave me other life priorities. I couldn't justify the expense of new clubs that might get used once a month. But once my kids got older and went to college my golf fever returned. But here's the key—only when I committed to playing more golf - stage 3 - did I commit to buy new clubs. So how did I decide what to buy?

I've played golf since I was a toddler and competed at a national level during college. Back then I played Ben Hogan irons. After deciding to buy something I started to look seriously at what was on the market. I learned that the Hogan company was making golf clubs again after several years of being out of business. I have to admit I got a little sentimental. Should I play Hogans again?

First, I defined my decision criteria. Should I play a cavity back style or a forged blade? Should I use standard shafts or light weight ones? Should I replace the 3-iron with a hybrid? Once I got beyond those important considerations then I shopped for brand. Though I considered several brands and models, I bought the Hogans. Was I trying to relive my glory days? Darned right I was!

Here's another example of how emotional the buying process can be. A client of mine in the commercial HVAC business often sells major systems to schools in Texas. A school might need to improve infrastructure or expand classroom capacity. Since this is a high-profile and public exercise, the buying process has to be transparent. But even in these types of sales there's a lot of emotion on the part of the customer. For example, wouldn't it be reasonable to think that someone on the buying committee might want to avoid picking a risky solution to avoid being seen as reckless with the tax payer's money? Those tax payers could be sitting next to that school official in church on Sunday.

Am I saying that everyone is so methodical and careful when they buy something? No. But remember that the purpose of the model is for you—the seller—not the buyer. Use it to know the questions you need to be asking about the buying journey and you'll be more effective at selling.

Blindspots: The Hidden Killer of Sales Coaching

You can use the model to understand better if a customer is putting more emotion than logic into a purchase, or vice versa. You can understand better how important the business impact is to committing to buying something from someone. You can understand how methodical, or loose, the customer is in defining the decision criteria. To be clear, on those occasions where the customer is not including some criteria that you know is important to include—not just because this favors your solution but it's the right approach to the problem—the model alerts you to this. You can advise the customer that something's missing in what he said was important and be seen as someone who's looking out for him.

The Hogan salesperson who sold to me by phone was overall helpful but missed the emotional part of my buying process. He helped me with the logical considerations like shaft weight, style of head, lie and loft. But he didn't ask me anything about my game or history. That's a big miss because often it's that emotional component that's the tiebreaker between options, or it's the 'stage boost' that accelerates the buying process. Though it didn't affect the outcome for him, it nonetheless is something to not ignore.

The BuyCycle Funnel™ Model Help Sales Teams Hit Quota

At the end of the day you want a greater number of your salespeople hitting quota. Aberdeen Consulting found that companies that use buying journey models have more salespeople hitting quota. The BuyCycle Funnel™ model impacts this in several ways.

For one, it's not a selling method; it's a sales model that makes selling methods more effective. Whatever selling methods you use (Miller Heiman, Challenger, SPIN, Wilson, TAS, Complex Sale, Solution Selling, Rain Selling, Richardson, Carew, IMPAX, etc.), the BuyCycle Funnel™ will make them more effective by giving the salesperson context. For example, a salesperson shouldn't have the same call plan for a customer who is 57% through his buying process (stage 3 or 4) that he would have for a customer who is 5% through his buying process. He wouldn't have the same call plan for a PFA (Person with Financial Authority) who has yet to "commit to buy" as he would have for a PFA who has made that commitment. The BuyCycle Funnel™ model tells you the customer is 57% through the buying process, or they're barely at stage 1.

The BuyCycle Funnel™ helps sellers hit quota by keeping their funnels accurate. There's less artificial inflation of funnel value (TVR, Total Viable Revenue). It tells the salesperson clearly if he has enough TVR or not and how to go about getting more. It also helps by defining selling priorities, one of the biggest challenges in sales.

The BuyCycle Funnel also helps managers hold their sales people accountable to the selling priorities that salespeople commit to week after week, month after month. While some sellers tend to complain and resist when their managers hold them accountable, they sometimes need someone to keep them focused. And having no accountability is rarely an option. The sales manager must know that the important work is getting done, or not.

The BuyCycle Funnel™ Model Creates Accurate Forecasts

Not a week goes by when I hear about a sales leader or CEO grumble about poor forecasting. The BuyCycle Funnel™ addresses this in several ways.

First, it defines the right stage for the opportunity. This fixes the most common and costly mistake salespeople make in managing the funnel. When deals are placed at the right stage, the funnel is accurate, and an accurate funnel leads to an accurate forecast.

Second, instead of using weighted stage values, the BuyCycle Funnel™ gives the manager TVR, Total Viable Revenue. While not all TVR is included in the forecast, the forecast comes from deals that are

TVR because they've passed the critical threshold of committing to buy something from someone.

By deploying The BuyCycle Funnel across all sales regions, companies reduce forecast variability. The framework rolls up from the salesperson through the front line managers to their supervisor, and on up to the CEO, president or owner. It's the equivalent of all of the musicians playing to the same timing. It makes for great music.

Changing the Coaching Conversation

The net net of the BuyCycle Funnel™ is that it makes for more effective opportunity management and strategies and more effective sales funnel management. For many sales managers it changes the deal and funnel conversations that they have with their salespeople. Instead of solely focusing on seller actions, managers are focused on the buyer commitments their salespeople need to get. Instead of letting selling activity determine funnel value, the BuyCycle Funnel™ confirms that customers have committed to buying something from someone— it's now documented funnel value. It's focusing on understanding the buying process and what the salesperson knows and has yet to find out.

While I've never heard anyone tell me that the customer buying journey concept didn't make sense, focusing selling attention on it is not easy. Many have even said it's intuitive. In my experience just because something's intuitive doesn't mean it becomes the default, or muscle memory. Like many things involving change, it's sometimes hard for salespeople and their managers to trust the simplicity of the BuyCycle Funnel model. If you commit to this concept for your coaching, you'll find it makes a profound impact.

9

The Funnel Audit™ Conversation

"Sales is just a conversation with a close."
– Steve Maragakes, Mark's first sales manager
after college, at Johnson & Johnson

One of the most important sales processes you can have is one that focuses on the sales funnel. Many well-known research and sales consulting firms have consistently found that companies that have well-defined, disciplined processes for the sales funnel perform at higher levels than do the companies without these processes.

Talking to sales leaders, one could think they've got this base covered. Nearly every sales leader I meet tells me, "Mark, we talk about the pipeline all the time." I listen. I learn. Often I discover they think they're talking about the funnel when they're really talking about something else. Remember Dave's $36M funnel in an earlier chapter? He talked about the funnel all the time. Then how did he miss by a mile what his region's funnel health was?

Blindspots: The Hidden Killer of Sales Coaching

Being good in sales or being a sales manager for eight years or 22 years or 40 years, or even being the Vice President of Sales doesn't endow people with gifts of leading effective sales funnel conversations. Talent and experience are not sufficient. Nothing replaces intentional practice and effort to improve. When sales funnel conversations are approached the right way, both the salesperson and manager greatly benefit. One way to do this is through the Funnel Audit™.

The Funnel Audit™ Conversation

The Funnel Audit is a structured, monthly 1:1 conversation between the sales manager and salesperson. There are two purposes:

- Determine the health of the sales funnel
- Create a 30-day plan of action

These two purposes should be enough to explain why Funnel Audits™ are important. When salespeople know the funnel health, and when they consistently define their selling priorities (the 30-day plan), they're more likely to achieve their ultimate objective, to hit quota. Having these conversations on a cadence throughout the year keeps sellers on track.

There are three parts to the Audit—the Dashboard, What's Changed, and the 30-Day Plan.

Dashboard

The dashboard is a static snapshot of key metrics such as the salesperson's quota, year-to-date sales, and the quota gap. This tells the rep how much more she has to sell to hit quota. Obviously this is a good place to start.

We then need to know the funnel size, specifically if the funnel is big enough to close that quota gap. As mentioned before, we refer to funnel value as TVR, Total Viable Revenue. If a salesperson says she has $2,000,000 of TVR, that means her funnel value is $2,000,000. But

TVR isn't the only data we're looking for. We want to know if the TVR is *enough* to close the existing sales quota gap. Enough TVR is called Target TVR. If Target TVR is $4M and the funnel has $2M on it, well, that's not enough. This data is a good start for the conversation. Beyond the obvious (whether there's enough TVR or there's not enough TVR), these questions can drive good conversation such as:

You've got enough Target TVR, that's great. But I see you have two deals that make up 85% of your TVR value. Let's talk about that.

Or the opposite…

You've got enough Target TVR, that's great. But I see you have 27 deals that make up 85% of your TVR value. Let's talk about the challenges you might have in adequately covering 27 sales opportunities.

Or you might see that a funnel has no early stage deals. A typical question might be: *We know your funnel needs more TVR. With no early stage deals on your funnel what can we do to get more early stage opportunities soon?*

Though dashboard data is static and a lagging indicator, it can still help a sales manager diagnose a salesperson's activity and performance. For example, where does the rep stand regarding year-to-date quota? In general, you'd probably want a $1M territory to be at $250,000 of year-to-date sales by the end of Q1 right? And maybe at $500,000 by the 6-month mark. Based on seasonal or cyclical dynamics in your business, these milestones might be different but they at least give you a benchmark.

What's Changed

The second part of the Funnel Audit is called "what's changed." Knowing where and how the sales funnel is changing from month to month helps you coach your salesperson to define the right selling priorities. Since these Audits are done once a month we look back over the past 30 days to identify how the funnel has changed or not.

Blindspots: The Hidden Killer of Sales Coaching

For example, does the salesperson have more TVR than last month? Was getting more TVR part of last month's 30-day plan? Does he have more early-stage opportunities? That's good to know, especially if last month we identified the need for that. Did he close some sales? Did he lose some? Did any opportunities move stages?

This data helps you encourage conversation around *why* the funnel has changed, or not. You're able to help the rep connect the dots between the salesperson's activities and funnel movement. If a funnel is healthy and we can't link it to specific things the salesperson is doing, then how do we possibly coach the salesperson on what to keep doing and what to start doing and what to stop doing? What evidence do you have that the salesperson's good looking funnel isn't just luck?

Let's say a salesperson's funnel needs more early-stage deals. We might say she needs to prospect more. But what exactly are we going to coach her to do? We need to know what's the best use of her time in prospecting for more early-stage deals. We could start by learning the history of her early-stage leads that have been on her funnel in the past:

- Where did those leads come from? How many came from existing customers (upselling or increase share of customer opportunities)?
- How many came from new customers?
- Were these web-based leads, such as inquiries?
- Were they referrals?
- Were they trade show leads?
- What line of business are the leads for?
- Are they from the key accounts or from smaller ones?

Knowing what has changed always generates rich discussions and leads to lots of learning during the Funnel Audits.

The 30-Day Plan

The Funnel Audit conversation concludes by defining a 30-day plan of action. This might sound like a to-do list, something you already have, but there are some important differences.

Goals: The 30-day plan defines Goals the salesperson wants to accomplish. We distinguish between a Goal to be accomplished and an action to be done. Goals are things that your customer commits to doing. This is what defines movement on the funnel. Actions are what the salesperson does to accomplish the Goal. For example, a Goal would be to have a key stakeholder for one of your deals give you great coaching on how to proceed with your sales strategy. The action might be a prep call to the key stakeholder and creating a plan to talk to the stakeholder. Having a stakeholder help set up an important meeting between you and other key stakeholders would be a Goal. Having this meeting is a sign of movement or action. You still need specific things to happen as a result of the meeting, but you need the meeting first.

Alignment: The most important part of the 30-day plan is that it must be aligned with the health of the funnel. If the funnel needs more TVR, then that has to be part of the 30-day plan. If the funnel has too many viable opportunities to get to in the next 30 days, then the task is to identify the ones that are a priority. If the funnel has little activity at the early stages and that puts the rep at risk of not having enough TVR later, then adding more early-stage deals to the funnel is the mission.

Accountability: In the 30-day plan the sales manager has a simple, effective tool to hold his salespeople accountable. If you're like some of my clients that have five, six, seven or more salespeople reporting to you, you know how hard it can be to do this. And this is just one part of your job.

Each month the sales manager refers to the 30-day plans of each salesperson to see if they accomplished the things that count the most right now. These plans aren't defined and given by you; they are defined and owned by the salesperson. They are simply using you to hold them accountable to what they defined as important.

In a way the Funnel Audit™ is like the Weight Watcher's diet program. Each week the Weight Watcher steps on the scale to see how well he executed the plan over the past week or two. It's about being held accountable.

Give the Funnel Audit™ Call Context

One of the most important things a sales manager can do when preparing for the Funnel Audit coaching call is to give it context. In other words, whatever's happening in the salesperson's world right now must be part of the conversation. This is key because these calls happen every month like clockwork and they can easily be taken for granted. I see it happen all the time. The manager says, "Okay, let's go through your funnel," and there's no context at all to what's going on in the business. As a result the rep sometimes fails to see the relevance of this audit and how this conversation is key to where he commits his time and effort for the next 30 days.

Ironically, it's not hard to see how every Funnel Audit should be different each month. Think of how different a Funnel Audit call in February would be from one in July of the same year. Think of how different that Funnel Audit would be if the salesperson was at risk of missing plan than if she was likely to hit plan in the tenth month.

One of my sales manager clients put his Audit in context better than anyone. When he's leading a Funnel Audit conversation, it's obvious that he's taken the time to frame up this conversation, to give context to it. He carefully lays out and reviews the situation with the rep—almost like a story— and covers things such as where the rep is year to date with sales, where he is in the fiscal year, what factors are affecting the business now like a back order situation or a competitive threat, and he puts this Funnel Audit conversation in that context.

Perhaps more than anything else you do, putting context to these coaching calls will continue to make them—and you—relevant and valuable.

Avoid These Most Common Mistakes

As you've read this chapter you've probably been able to make a list of the common mistakes that sales managers make when leading sales funnel conversations. Let me make it easy for you with a list of don'ts.

Don't:

- Let the sales funnel conversation become a deal-review conversation.
- Make the Funnel Audit the same as what is discussed day to day and week to week with your salespeople.
- Allow the salesperson to dominate the audit by complaining about company problems.
- Do all the talking if you're the manager.
- Speak in theoretical terms—instead make it practical. Coach specifically to the funnel in front of you.
- As manager, neglect to take the time before the Audit to define the 2-3 things that this salesperson needs to be coached on and how to provide that coaching.
- Spend too much time nitpicking about what stage a deal is at on the funnel.
- Sound judgmental.
- Interrogate by asking question after question.
- Miss the opportunity to define the Goals of the 30-day plan.

Blindspots: The Hidden Killer of Sales Coaching

Simplify, Focus and Hold People Accountable

The intent of the Funnel Audit conversation is to empower the sales manager with a way to provide ongoing and consistent focus and drive accountability of net new sales. A day in the life of any salesperson is fraught with many distractions that divert focus from this. You'll help your salespeople in big ways by using a Funnel Audit approach to this vital function.

Part 3: Your Lifelong Battle with Blindspots

10

Don't Let Sales Process Be a Blindspot

"If you can see your path laid out in front of you step by step, you know it's not your path. Your own path you make with every step you take."
– Joseph Campbell, author and professor

If you've ever mis-hit a nail and had to take it back out with the claw end of the hammer, you know how a lever works. I hope your finger and thumb were spared.

I've noticed something about sales processes over the years. Some managers are absolutely brilliant at making them work. Like a lever. Others, not so brilliant. Like a liability. A lot of smashed thumbs.

Maybe it's not so surprising that the sales process, the very thing that is supposed to enable you as a sales manager, is something that can get in your way—another paradox and another potential blindspot. In this chapter I'll share with you some ideas to help you make your sales process a lever, stay out of your own way, and make an impact on sales performance.

Blindspots: The Hidden Killer of Sales Coaching

Sales Process Primer

Let's get aligned on what a sales process is. The dictionary defines "process" this way:

A series of actions or steps taken to achieve a particular end.

If we add "sales" to the front of that then it might sound like this:

A series of sales actions or steps taken to achieve a particular end.

Your company could have more than one sales process. For example, you could have a sales process for your pipeline with the specific end for that process being healthy sales funnels that are sufficient to achieving quota.

You could also have a sales process for how you have sales conversations with clients. The particular end might be some measure of progress made toward the sale as a result of the sales call. You could have a process for how you strategize for sales opportunities. This particular end might be making the sale, ultimately, but also might be making measurable progress, stage by stage, in the customer's buying process. And you could have a sales process for how you manage key or strategic accounts or for how you negotiate.

CRM and Sales Process

Clearly, there are many sales processes. Customer Relationship Management (CRM) has become synonymous with sales process, maybe due to a bias of thinking that process means something to do with computers. However, a company can have a sales process without a CRM system. I've seen some that work well. On the other hand, I've seen processes that are predominantly about the CRM that barely get off the ground. They're too bureaucratic and not user friendly. The salespeople don't benefit as much from these processes.

CRM can play a valuable role in sales process mainly with visibility, analysis and reporting.

Visibility

CRM helps sales managers and salespeople have visibility to the sales funnel. A Vice President of Sales can see territory funnels, region funnels, product or line of business funnels, and more. Visibility can roll up from the territory level all the way to the corner office. I've had several clients that set up this type of structure. Visibility makes it possible to have intelligent funnel conversations, because as they say in LEAN, if you can see it, you can change it.

However, visibility alone is insufficient. Visibility doesn't tell a manager where a rep is spending her time and how she is determining her sales priorities. Visibility doesn't help you understand what the data is trying to say about funnel health. What sales leaders need more than visibility is insight. What's the data mean? How do we analyze what we can see here?

Insight/Analysis

With our obsession for data comes a premium on analytics. Analytics help managers provide good coaching to their salespeople. For example, if you knew that one of your salespeople was 30% penetrated in a given key account and the market is growing at 8% per annum, you might coach her to defend and protect the position and still grow her sales. But if the market is flat, then any growth is likely to come only from a more aggressive penetration strategy. Without the analytic insight you could pay a price for taking the wrong strategy.

One of the problems of CRM is not really a fault of CRM. Visibility is not insight. Just because a manager can see the number of opportunities someone has at each funnel stage, it doesn't mean he understands it or that this visibility tells the whole story of the health of the rep's funnel. It's important to define those stages correctly (see BuyCycle Funnel chapter) and to have a cadence and process for calling out the "BS" in those funnels. With the "commit to buy something from somebody" stage of the BuyCycle Funnel, for example, a manager can distinguish between an opportunity that is not destined to become a sale versus an opportunity that is. That's insightful and helps the manager define priorities appropriately.

One of our clients in the specialty chemical industry used analytics a few years ago to focus their selling efforts on selling their higher-margin products. They isolated selling activity with the higher-margin products and found that this helped them sell more of them and achieve important results for both top and bottom lines. The strategy paid off handsomely.

Reporting

CRM is great for creating reports that drive conversation and strategy. Two different types of reports are those that give leading indicator insight and those that give lagging indicator insight.

A lagging indicator is one where the report is pulled from information that is less timely to act on. Sales reports are the most common lagging indicator. You can't do much about the data. It's in the books. You can still learn from sales data, such as sales trends that go up or down for a specific customer, or maybe the seasonality of a sales trend. But you can't do anything about this lagging data.

A leading indicator is one where the report provides information that could be timely to act on. The funnel value report is the best example of this. If the funnel for a rep's territory is weak and it's early in the year, you have time to act on that. With coaching you can help the rep develop a stronger funnel that will still impact this year's quota.

Remember the phrase regarding sales data —garbage in, garbage out. The reports are only as valuable as the data in them is accurate. And we know that many sales funnels are not 100% accurate due to many different reasons.

Sales Process Intent

The intent of sales process is the same as the intent of any process: to most efficiently achieve the particular end.

A sales process breaks down the work of selling into smaller parts and lets you know which parts are being performed well and which ones are not. For example, if you want to coach your salesperson to make really good sales calls, you would want to know where in the process she needs to improve and where you need to coach. Are her openings compelling enough? Does she ask the right kinds of questions at the right time? Does she build trust enough? Does she struggle to close? Or does she add a lot of new early-stage opportunities but fail to move them along the process? Does she give all opportunities the same priority and attention? If the answer is no, it's not good territory or funnel management.

Sales process helps drive out waste and increase effectiveness. When there's process, there's knowledge of what's working and what's not.

(Ironically) The Downside of Sales Process

The paradox of sales process is that it's supposed to make you and your salespeople more effective, but it has the potential to make you less effective. Sometimes, instead of becoming a lever, it becomes a liability. This book is about blindspots and the sales process can be a big one.

One reason for this is the challenge of CRM. Many executives experience the common problem of new CRM systems taking a lot of their salesforce's time to enter information and keep it up to date. "If it's not in salesforce, it's not real" is a cry I commonly hear from sales managers. Sales managers and their sellers complain that they're in front of the laptop screens more often than in front of customers.

Sometimes executives get too ambitious with their timeframes in using the CRM system. They've spent a lot of money on it and they want it to pay off now. Blindspot! I suggest a crawl-walk-run pace. I suggest a honeymoon period to give people a break on getting up to speed with the CRM demands.

Another reason that sales process can be a challenge is when it is too rigidly used by the sales managers. I've seen some sales managers rely so much on the process that it has become a crutch to their coaching. They expect the process to provide everything they need regarding information and context into opportunities and funnels. They've forgotten or never learned to have conversations with their people. It might be the equivalent of the manager who never gets out in the field with his or her people and who "runs" the region entirely from the laptop.

Stop Assuming Your People Understand the Purpose of the Process

Sales leaders can mislead themselves into thinking how well their sales teams understand the reasons for implementing sales process. Making a kickoff announcement is often not sufficient. You should consider communicating from every level of your sales organization. The Vice President or head of sales has a message. The directors reinforce it with their message. The sales managers do the same directly with their people.

I sat in on a sales process coaching call with a client of mine recently where the new sales manager asked his salesperson, "Would you say this worksheet is more for you or for management?" The salesperson candidly replied, "More for management."

Getting buy-in to the sales process is important. When we run the BuyCycle Funnel design workshop the client's subject matter experts— their salespeople and their managers—are co-creating the process with us. These workshop participants spread the word with their colleagues later about the value of the process. This makes a strong impression. Creating a sales advisory council is another way to communicate the purpose of a sales process change and how it will affect the stakeholders in the company.

Don't Go Overboard Selling the WIIFM

Executives sometimes spend too much time on the WIIFM for salespeople—What's In It For Me—and not enough time being brutally transparent about the benefit to the entire enterprise. It's worse when the WIIFM rhetoric is all about how the salespeople will benefit. Instead, appeal to the common sense of your salesforce. The business has needs that the sales process or CRM investment will address. Stakeholders, aside from the salespeople, will benefit from it. The more transparent you can be, and the more honest you can be about the purpose of the sales process, the more they'll likely understand the need to change even if they aren't thrilled with what it means for them.

Have a Change Strategy

Believe it or not it's common to see sales leaders go into a big sales process change initiative and not have a plan that deals with reasonable resistance. And yet they know it's going to come. It's reasonable to be hesitant to change—for several reasons. These include not wanting to lose face, not wanting too much uncertainty, not wanting to be surprised, not wanting to be seen as incompetent to make the change, and others. By planning for this resistance, you'll be more successful at getting people to buy into the change.

Your plan should include plenty of listening and letting your people know you hear them. Sometimes that's all it takes. Sometimes we're tempted to think that if we shove it hard down their throats as quickly as possible, it won't come back up. Along with not fast-tracking buy in, a hard sell can backfire sometimes.

Blindspots: The Hidden Killer of Sales Coaching

Change Will Likely Evolve

There's a line in the song, "Tom Sawyer," by the Canadian rock band Rush where Geddy Lee screams, "He knows changes aren't permanent, but change is."

The mistake some executives make when implementing a sales process is they don't tell their teams to expect evolving changes to the process. If a team believes that change is a one-time event, like attending a training workshop, but in reality will be continuous, they could become frustrated or annoyed and you'll risk losing credibility for the program.

Use the Process to Have Good Conversations

I recall a speech I heard given by the CEO of a major chemical company who said he spends more time preparing for the individual conversations he has with his staff members than the time it takes to have those conversations. He says he can't be too careful because people can misunderstand something or try to read something into what he's saying. And since he's the CEO people will put a lot of weight to what he says.

When you think of the best coaching conversations you have had with your salespeople—like the best learning conversations you have had with your kids—they often happen when it's just a great conversation.

Sometimes the structure around these coaching conversations, meant to add value, creates an artificial obstacle that sends people into lock-down mode, and it becomes a value killer. I'm not suggesting you discard structure. The key to making these calls effective is to make sure they are conversations. You must get good enough with the structure so that they come off simply as conversations.

Some of the most ineffective Funnel Audit conversations I hear occur when the manager lets the structure of the Audit hijack the conversation. The focus should be on the funnel, not the process. Avoiding this becomes one of our most important coaching topics.

I coach the managers to think of the framework as having boundaries which are guideposts to help us exercise good judgment. Within the boundaries is space for being flexible and creative. Compare it to any developed country's system of road travel. There are speed limits, lines on the road to indicate permissible behavior like passing, and signs to warn drivers. But if it's snowing or raining hard, you might find yourself going 35mph in a 45mph zone. Or candidly, you might go 75mph on a remote highway that has a 70mph limit and not risk getting a ticket. You exercise judgment.

If a sales manager leading a Funnel Audit finds herself 15 minutes into a 12-minute budgeted time to discuss a few key deals because the conversation is leading to some excellent dialogue and learning, I say keep at it. As long as 15 minutes doesn't become 30 and steal from the other sections of the Audit conversation, it's okay. On the flip side, if deal discussions during a Funnel Audit take nine minutes because there are no more deals to discuss, why drag it out?

Be Sensitive to Venue

A healthy venue promotes a healthy coaching conversation. When my clients have Funnel Audits with their salespeople every month, you can expect that sometimes the venues aren't ideal. We've had Audits with reps pulled into rest stops, gas stations, hospital lobbies, and construction sites. We always ask if they're in a safe place. Sometimes they've got their laptops open and sometimes they're using their phones to see the data and to talk. I admire their commitment to the process, but if there's a pattern with any of your salespeople where they always seem to be on the run when having these cadence calls, that's probably getting in the way of maximizing the value of those calls. It's possible the salesperson doesn't take the process as seriously as you'd like. You might try to find some other way of making the cadence call more of a priority.

Prepare for the Coaching Conversation

Another client of mine thought that her good intentions on her coaching conversations would be understood by her salespeople, even when her style of communicating the intent was not ideal. I disagreed and told her so. First, I suggested that she has far too much hope that her salespeople are able to read her mind. Second, people are more likely to think something negative or wrong than positive and right. A friend of mine expresses this well. She says when her CEO leaves her a message and says, "We need to talk," which is more than occasional, she immediately thinks she did something wrong or she's getting fired, even though she's highly regarded by him!

Make Your People Comfortable

Remember, the transparency of sales data is a proven cause of discomfort and tension on sales process calls. And blindspots. It's easy to see how these calls can make a salesperson nervous.

There can be additional reasons for this discomfort. The manager and salesperson might have a rocky relationship. The manager could be unnecessarily and even unknowingly exercising his dominant authority position over the salesperson. If it's a call to inspect funnel health and the funnel isn't healthy, the rep might want to crawl under the table and hide. If the salesperson doesn't feel competent to follow the process, he's uncomfortably exposed. If the manager has blindspots regarding the salesperson's discomfort in these calls, then anything the manager does can unintentionally throw fuel on the fire. If the salesperson is not open to any coaching or has a negative feeling about the manager, the salesperson is never giving anything the sales manager does any chance of being constructive.

Sales Processes Aren't Going Away

You're likely to see more attention given to process regarding your company's selling efforts. The intentions are usually good, but intentions alone won't make sales processes effective and good intentions often reek of blindspots. Giving careful consideration to workflow, reporting, the pace of change, venue, and the impact on the people using it— mainly your salespeople—will go a long way in creating unforced errors. It will also go a long way at making your sales process initiative a success.

11

You Need to Be Coached

"You cannot architect your own transformation."
– Richard Rohr, author of *Falling Upward*

"You can't make it in Dublin, Ohio by yourself."
– Mark Van Huffel, men's spirituality group leader,
St. Brigid of Kildare church Dublin, Ohio

Though I don't know you, I know you need to be coached. And I bet that you had a blindspot or two that you were unaware of when you started this book. Since you've made it this far in the book, I know a little about you. I know you're well above average in all that you do. You aim high and work hard. You're always looking for an edge to get better in everything you do. You make sacrifices to achieve your goals.

By now I hope you realize that because you are human you have blindspots that prevent you from becoming a better sales manager and person. I've shown you why blindspots are particularly challenging. The paradox of the blindspot can be hard to understand. Though you can't rewire yourself, you can become more self-aware of how your wiring drives your motivations and behaviors.

When it comes to self-awareness, it's tempting to believe that you are the reason for where you are and what you've achieved. It's tempting to believe that your hard work is your work alone. It's tempting to believe that by rising early and staying late too many times to count, that by putting in your 10,000 hours, that by sacrificing one thing to achieve another, that by delaying gratification to get long term rewards, you've made it happen. These were your choices and you own them. And you reap what you have sown. Let me be clear—I celebrate your decisions and results!

But consider this: by definition, you are the product of the relationships and associations of your life. All of them. The ones you had no control over and the ones that your wise decisions have created. It is tempting to give ourselves more credit in what we've accomplished and who we have become. This is unhealthy ego standing tall and proud.

While it's your race to run, you don't run it alone. As you go through your arc of life, your continued growth depends on you becoming more aware of your blindspots. Aging is no guarantee of growing wiser. We've all probably met older people who behave like children. And perhaps you've met youth who are wise beyond their years. As we age it's natural to settle into patterned, grooved ways of thinking and behaving. The energy required to push ourselves out of the cozy chair of our mindset can be hard to summon. Your blindspots can take deeper root. They can multiply and expand.

But it's also natural to become more open to different possibilities. The first step toward getting out of your own way is often to embrace a fall. For me it was Singapore. Eventually, I decided to embrace being wounded and had the courage to be patient to learn what it was trying to teach me. I also had people come into my life who gave me timely advice and counsel when I asked for it. A good friend of mine gave me a couple of books to read that rocked my paradigm. This began the new journey.

Humility comes flying in like an emotional SWAT crew when you finally embrace the fall instead of fighting it. The journey that humility will take you on is nothing short of liberating and eye opening.

If, as of this reading, you don't think you've fallen and been wounded, then the next step is to look for your blindspots in the right place—your virtues. Remember, your blindspots are hidden in plain view. The very traits and characteristics that propelled you to success will someday betray you. Likely more than once. But know, too, that this betrayal is the gift. It's pushing you to have the courage to let some small part of yourself die. I can't tell you what that is for you. Only you can.

Richard Rohr says it is virtually impossible to architect our own transformation. Just because I've explained the concept of blindspots, and given you my own personal story of how my virtues became my vices, and told you the stories and examples of my clients and their blindspots, you might still not be convinced that you need to change. So know that we have to be summoned. When ready, we have to be the student for whom the teacher will show up. We need to steer clear of our blindspots.

Lest this sound like you have no control over being transformed, let me correct that. You can do something right now. Take some time to take an inventory of some things. Anything less than brutal honesty is prolonging the suffering. Ask yourself these questions:

- ✓ What's most important in my life?
- ✓ Why is that?
- ✓ What am I most afraid of?
- ✓ Do I really know how I come across to people?
- ✓ Do I care?
- ✓ What would people say candidly about me if there were no

repercussions?
- ✓ What do I covet?
- ✓ Am I aware of when my pride turns ugly?
- ✓ Whom do I envy?
- ✓ What gets me angry?
- ✓ How do I behave when I'm angry?

Before you think I'm standing in a glass house throwing stones at you, remember that this drill sergeant has been through the same boot camp that he's encouraging you to attend. I know unflattering behavior because I practiced it daily for years. I know how to pass judgment because I became very good at it. I know what's self-centered. I looked in the mirror. I guess you could say I now have written the book on all of this!

Where Do You Begin to Get Out of Your Own Way?

The writer Anne Lamott wrote in her book, *Bird by Bird*, that *"good writing is about telling the truth."* She also tells the story of her brother, who, when tasked with writing a report on birds, lamented, *"I have no idea where to begin."* Her father sat down beside him, put his arm on her brother's shoulder, and said, *"Bird by bird, buddy. Just take it bird by bird."*

I think this student is not alone. Finding the place to start is often daunting. But in the well-worn words of a Chinese proverb, "A journey of a thousand miles begins with a single step." It also begins with the truth.

Truth, in and of itself, seems simple. Maybe it is for some. In my experience it can be hard to find. While truth always makes itself visible, our eyes don't always see it clearly.

I find truth is sometimes hard because honesty is the key to unlock it, and with honesty comes pain. Churchill's painting was too honest for him. Frasier couldn't trade honesty for all that he coveted. I suppressed my feelings for years.

In their wonderful book, *The Art of the Nudge*, Chris Miles and John Geraci describe change as being like a dirt road or a superhighway. They say we resist changing because we prefer to keep traveling the well-paved, well-lighted, safe, familiar roads of the super highways. To change is like taking the exit for the unpaved, rocky, dirt road. We don't know what's around the corner because we can't see around the corner. But like a curious traveler soon discovers, sometimes the best experiences are those that are not planned.

No one should be blamed for staying on the superhighway. But also think about your future and consider beginning with a small change. Consider any of the following actions to nudge you to getting out of your own way:

- ✓ Hire a personal coach.
- ✓ See your priest or pastor or rabbi or imam.
- ✓ Join a small faith group.
- ✓ Give your witness talk.
- ✓ See a therapist.
- ✓ Break a pattern in your life that's not serving you well.
- ✓ Volunteer.
- ✓ Join a service organization and commit time to a project.
- ✓ Acknowledge a bias or prejudice without judging yourself.
- ✓ Forgive. Yourself and others.

When I traveled to Mumbai, Shanghai, and Singapore on business years ago, all on one trip, I got lots of advice before leaving. In Singapore, go see the Marina Bay at night. It's stunning. In Shanghai, be sure to visit the Bund. Get off of the main commercial roads, too, and see the sidewalk vendors selling fish, fruits, produce, hardware goods, etc. The advice I got for Mumbai? Well, said one well-traveled client of mine, don't eat anything. Don't drink the water. Bring a bunch of energy bars. He laughed when I told him I was going during the rainy season.

It turned out that while I enjoyed the first two cities, Mumbai was the jewel. Maybe it was a combination of the funny, animated and engaged Indian sales team I trained and hung with for three days; their proud hospitality as they took me to the Gateway to India, Leopold Café, and Juhu Beach at midnight; the fabulous food; the alphonso mangos, better than ice cream; the remarkable traffic sights. I'm thankful I was open to the possibilities.

Virtue v. Vice, Again

Your virtues, when they descend into vices, are a formidable opponent. They do what they're wired to do. They don't know any better. In a way your virtues are like an auto immune disease. Auto immune diseases, such as rheumatoid arthritis or multiple sclerosis, are devastating. The immune system thinks it's working as it is supposed to. It doesn't realize it is attacking healthy cells by mistake, causing severe damage.

Here's a crazy conversation I imagine going on between the attacking immune system and some central command center that knows that what's going on is wrong.

Central command: *Hey immune system! Can't you see what you're doing? Stop killing those healthy cells. You have no idea what harm you are causing!*

Immune system: *I don't know what you're talking about. I've been attacking my whole life. I was made to attack. You're alive because I attack!*

Central command: *I know you've protected me well but sometimes your attacking works against me. Just because you've always been an attacker doesn't mean you always have to be an attacker. Let's put* *your skills to use doing something else.*

Immune system: *Attacking is who I am. I've made my name by attacking. Stop talking to me. I have more attacking to do.*

With these terrible autoimmune diseases it's a paradox: the immune system's instincts do not realize they are slowly destroying what is good.

I've shared my story in many different words in this book. I found help in an unlikely place for me—a church group. For me the help came in the form of men like me, sharing their stories of struggles and challenges. We get together regularly in the spirit of brotherhood, anchored in our faith. We share a lot. We discover that our issues are common. I learned that my pain was no more or less special than the next guy's. But we now have a connection. And as Brené Brown said in the *Ted Talk* we are all striving for connection in this life and world.

In his book, *The Power of the Other*, Dr. Henry Cloud reveals the science behind connection and depending on others. It was an unexpected key ingredient for me to overcome my vice-type behaviors and to become more of who I was destined to be. His advice goes against conventional thought. Often, his high-achieving clients think they can get out of their own way by focusing on or leveraging their own strengths. *If I work harder... if I am more disciplined... if I just resist this addictive urge again ... if I control my impulses....*

The problems, however, are not caused by strengths, but rather by weaknesses. A solution that doesn't address the weaknesses is doomed to fail. This is the cornerstone of the 12 Steps for Alcoholics Anonymous too. You reach the point of your own helplessness and then have a decision to make. Reach for the hand that's extended to help you or deny your condition and stay imprisoned. When I admitted I couldn't control my way out of my situation and needed the help of others, I began to heal. These were not muscles I used during my entire life. I had to embrace the contradiction. Man, it was hard.

Maybe you're thinking, That's great, I'm happy for you Mark, but I'm not you. I don't have the problems you had. I don't need a coach or a therapist or a church or anybody to tell me what I have to do.

I respect your view. Though I don't know your story, I know I had similar feelings. Consider putting more intention to what I've introduced you to. Go grab a cup of coffee with someone who you believe will respect your privacy and be honest with you about you. Try to avoid judging. Consider taking the Enneagram test (look for a link in the resources section or see our webpage). This test can provide powerful insights to help you become more self-aware.

If you are not used to being coached, or not used to seeking advice you will struggle. If you're a fighter, then like my success trait of discipline you could continue to mislead yourself. Beware of the vice in the virtue.

As you can guess I am fascinated with the stories of the men and women warriors who fell, suffered, learned from it, and then rose again. One of those stories is Tiger Woods. Most of us will never know the degree of intensity and dedication it took for Tiger to accomplish what he did. He is arguably the greatest golfer of all time. He is intense and focused. But his virtues became devastating vices. He fell hard. He lost his family, his marriage, friends, professional associations, endorsements. He lost confidence. Eventually, his body broke. But he was courageous in his patience to learn what the lesson was meant to teach him. Now he's become someone, including other players, who others enjoy being around and spending time with. He was a key coach for the U.S. Ryder Cup victory at Hazeltine in 2016.

Did it really take a broken soul to arrive at his new place? For him it did. But don't miss the larger point. Wouldn't it be a tragedy if his soul broke and he learned nothing from it?

Blindspots: The Hidden Killer of Sales Coaching

It's truly an amazing world we live in. If you're fortunate to find yourself in a part of the world where you have everything you need every day to eat abundantly, to sleep in comfort and safety, to feed your mental growth, to exercise your rights and freedom, to not be oppressed, to worship as you please, to have your physical and mental gifts intact, then give thanks, literally. Go find someone to thank. You didn't arrive in this place by yourself.

Continue to set your bar high. Work hard. Sacrifice. Apply your talents. Start working on a part of you that might have been neglected. Become more self-aware. Selfishly serve others. Practice humility every day. Gather your Corner 4 team.

It's your race, and you can't run it alone.

Resources

Adamson, Brent and Dixon, Matthew – *The Challenger Sale*

Brown, Brené – *Braving the Wilderness, The Gifts of Imperfection, Daring Greatly*

Boyle, Father Gregory – *Tattoos on the Heart, Barking to the Choir*

Dyer, Wayne – *Change Your Thoughts, Change Your Life, There's a Spiritual Solution to Every Problem, Manifest Your Destiny, You'll See It When You Believe It*

Cloud, Henry – everything, and in particular *Necessary Endings, The Power of the Other, Integrity*

Davis, Seth – *Wooden: A Coach's Life*

Eliot, TS – *The Love Song of J. Alfred Prufrock*

Heiman, Steve and Miller, Robert –*Conceptual Selling*

Keller, Tim – *The Reason for God, Making Sense of God, The Prodigal Prophet*

Kelly, Matthew – *The Four Pillars of a Dynamic Catholic*

Lamott, Anne – *Bird by Bird*

Martin, Father James – *Jesus, A Pilgrimage, My Life with the Saints*

Maxwell, John – *Everyone Communicates, Few Connect*

Merton, Thomas – *Seven Story Mountain*

Osteen, Joel – *You Can You Will*

Pable, Father Martin – *The Quest for the Male Soul*

Peterson, Eugene – *Run With the Horses, A Long Obedience in the Same Direction*

Riso, Don Richard and Hudson, Russ – *The Wisdom of the Enneagram*

Rohr, Richard – *Falling Upward, Immortal Diamond, Breathing Under Water*

Rubin, Gretchen – *The Happiness Project, The 4 Tendencies*

Sellers, Mark – *The Funnel Principle*

About Mark Sellers

For nearly 25 years and throughout this spectacular world, Mark Sellers has been coaching and training sales leaders, from front line managers up to presidents, owners, GMs and CEOs at companies ranging from $20M to $500M in sales. His company, Breakthrough Sales Performance, markets and sells its services globally through a network of sales consultants.

Sellers' first book, The Funnel Principle, was called "revolutionary" by *Selling Power* magazine. To date, hundreds of sales teams around the world have implemented The Funnel Principle selling system.

Mark is the proud father of three tax-paying children. He lives in Ohio with his wife Bonnie of 30 years, their rescue dog Dempsey whose tail does not stop wagging, and Louie, a ten-pound Chihuahua who, like Sinatra, does everything his way.

www.breakthrough-sales.com
blindspotsinsales.blog
614.571.8267

Expand Your Leadership & Coaching
with services from Breakthrough Sales Performance

Breakthrough Sales Performance offers additional ways to understand and manage your blindspots and expand the impact of your leadership. Go to *www.breakthrough-sales.com* or call 614.571.8267 to learn more.

Coaching to The Funnel Principle Selling System
This is a one day classroom based course for front line sales managers and their supervisors. You will learn how to lead effective sales funnel and deal conversations, learn a simple, powerful way to analyze the health of the sales funnel, learn effective ways of holding salespeople accountable, and learn to improve sales forecast accuracy.

Executive Coaching for Leaders of Businesses
This is a 6-month remote based program of coaching for senior leaders of businesses including GMs, presidents, CEOs and C-suite executives.

Keynote Speaking
Mark provides keynote speeches to help executives and teams to help them understand and deal with their blindspots.